Angular Design Patte

Implement the Gang of Four patterns in your apps with Angular

Mathieu Nayrolles

BIRMINGHAM - MUMBAI

Angular Design Patterns

Commissioning Editor: Ashwin Nair
Acquisition Editor: Rahul Nair
Content Development Editor: Aditi Gour
Technical Editor: Jinesh Topiwala
Copy Editor: Safis Editing
Project Coordinator: Hardik Bhinde
Proofreader: Safis Editing
Indexers: Mariammal Chettiyar
Graphics: Jason Monteiro
Production Coordinator: Shraddha Falebhai

First published: July 2018

Production reference: 1270718

Published by Packt Publishing Ltd.
Livery Place
35 Livery Street
Birmingham
B3 2PB, UK.

ISBN 978-1-78646-172-8

www.packtpub.com

`mapt.io`

Mapt is an online digital library that gives you full access to over 5,000 books and videos, as well as industry leading tools to help you plan your personal development and advance your career. For more information, please visit our website.

Why subscribe?

- Spend less time learning and more time coding with practical eBooks and Videos from over 4,000 industry professionals

- Improve your learning with Skill Plans built especially for you

- Get a free eBook or video every month

- Mapt is fully searchable

- Copy and paste, print, and bookmark content

PacktPub.com

Did you know that Packt offers eBook versions of every book published, with PDF and ePub files available? You can upgrade to the eBook version at `www.PacktPub.com` and as a print book customer, you are entitled to a discount on the eBook copy. Get in touch with us at `service@packtpub.com` for more details.

At `www.PacktPub.com`, you can also read a collection of free technical articles, sign up for a range of free newsletters, and receive exclusive discounts and offers on Packt books and eBooks.

About the author

Mathieu Nayrolles was born in France and lived in a small village in Côte d'Azur for almost 15 years. He started his computer science studies in France and continued in Montréal, Canada, where he now lives with his wife. Mathieu holds a PhD in electrical and computer engineering from Concordia University and two master degrees from eXia.Cesi (software engineering) and UQAM (computer science).

Despite his academic journey, Mathieu also worked for worldwide companies such as Ubisoft, Eurocopter, Ericsson, or Saint-Gobain, where he learned how important good technical resources are.

You can discover some of his works through his books: *Expert Angular, Xamarin Studio for Android Programming: A C# Cookbook, Mastering Apache Solr: A practical guide to get to grips with Apache Solr, Instant Magento Performances, Magento Performance Optimization: How to,* and *Mastering Apache.*

About the reviewer

Rajesh Gunasundaram is a software architect, technical writer, and blogger. He has over 15 years of experience in the IT industry. He is a founder and editor of technical blogs programmerguide [dot] net and ioscorner [dot] com. He has also written many books for Packt publishing and has a YouTube channel named ProgrammerGuide.

His technical strengths include Azure, Xamarin, ASP.NET MVC, Web API, WCF, .Net Framework / .Net Core, C#, Objective-C, Angular, Bot Framework, BizTalk, SQL Server, REST, SOA, design patterns and software architecture, Bootstrap, HTML5, and CSS3. He has also developed mobile applications. His expertise is in handling RESTful services in Angular.

Packt is searching for authors like you

If you're interested in becoming an author for Packt, please visit `authors.packtpub.com` and apply today. We have worked with thousands of developers and tech professionals, just like you, to help them share their insight with the global tech community. You can make a general application, apply for a specific hot topic that we are recruiting an author for, or submit your own idea.

Table of Contents

Preface

Angular by Google is a framework for building web applications. It is a completely new product as compared to AngularJS.

AngularJS was known to have performances issues, and it's not necessarily very easy to get started with. Everything could go well as long as you knew the very specifics and potential bottlenecks of the framework. In addition, AngularJS was often seen as a big toolbox, with a lot of tools inside, letting you build applications in many different ways, ending in various implementations of the same logic depending on the developer.

Angular brings tremendous improvements performance-wise, while being a much simpler and straightforward framework to use. Angular simply allows you to do more with less.

Google has announced from the start of the development of Angular that the framework would be a whole new product and wouldn't be compatible with AngularJS, while they might try to offer some tools to ease the transition. Often, rewriting your application from scratch might be the best solution to migrate it. In that context, it will be necessary for the developer to learn the key parts of the Angular framework in order to bootstrap an application and the best practices to develop it as well as the existing tools to debug and benchmark the application.

Taking a complete journey through the most valuable design patterns and providing clear guidance on how to effectively use them in Angular, this book gives you access to one of the best ways to learn Angular and use it to meet stability and quality required in today's web development.

We will take the reader on a journey across Angular designs for the real world with a combination of case studies, design patterns to follow, and anti-patterns to avoid.

By the end of the book, you will have learned about the various features of Angular and be able to apply well-known, industry-proven design patterns in your work.

Who this book is for

This book is for new Angular developers that want to increase their understanding of Angular and apply it to real-life application development.

What this book covers

Chapter 1, *TypeScript Best Practices*, describes some of the best practices of the Typescript language. While Angular is compatible with other programming languages, in this book, we use Typescript. Typescript is powerful and expressive, but there are a few *gotchas* to avoid.

Chapter 2, *Angular Bootstrapping*, allows us to start on the right foot using the best available tools to create, build, and deploy our applications.

Chapter 3, *Classical Patterns*, revisits some of the well-known object-oriented patterns within the context of Angular.

Chapter 4, *Navigational Patterns*, focuses on the different ways to navigate Angular apps.

Chapter 5, *Stability Patterns*, presents different stability patterns that can be used to ensure the stability of real-world Angular applications.

Chapter 6, *Performances Patterns*, builds on the huge performance improvements made to Angular by Google and describes applicable patterns to improve the performances of your applications.

Chapter 7, *Operation Patterns*, focuses on getting our applications as operations ready after having implemented our features using well-known design patterns and livening them with some performances and stability patterns.

To get the most out of this book

To get the most out of this book, the reader will need to know about Angular, Typescript, and object-oriented programming.

Download the example code files

You can download the example code files for this book from your account at www.packtpub.com. If you purchased this book elsewhere, you can visit www.packtpub.com/support and register to have the files emailed directly to you.

You can download the code files by following these steps:

1. Log in or register at `www.packtpub.com`.
2. Select the **SUPPORT** tab.
3. Click on **Code Downloads & Errata**.
4. Enter the name of the book in the **Search** box and follow the onscreen instructions.

Once the file is downloaded, please make sure that you unzip or extract the folder using the latest version of:

- WinRAR/7-Zip for Windows
- Zipeg/iZip/UnRarX for Mac
- 7-Zip/PeaZip for Linux

The code bundle for the book is also hosted on GitHub at `https://github.com/PacktPublishing/Angular-Design-Patterns`. We also have other code bundles from our rich catalog of books and videos available at `https://github.com/PacktPublishing/`. Check them out!

Download the color images

We also provide a PDF file that has color images of the screenshots/diagrams used in this book. You can download it here: `http://www.packtpub.com/sites/default/files/downloads/AngularDesignPatterns_ColorImages.pdf`.

Conventions used

There are a number of text conventions used throughout this book.

`CodeInText`: Indicates code words in text, database table names, folder names, filenames, file extensions, pathnames, dummy URLs, user input, and Twitter handles. Here is an example: "`APIService`, which displays the `@Injectable()` annotation that makes it, well, injectable."

A block of code is set as follows:

```
interface Animal{
    eat():void;
    sleep():void;
}
```

When we wish to draw your attention to a particular part of a code block, the relevant lines or items are set in bold:

```
ReferenceError: window is not defined
```

Any command-line input or output is written as follows:

```
$ curl -sL https://deb.nodesource.com/setup_6.x | sudo -E bash -
$ sudo apt-get install -y Node.js
```

Bold: Indicates a new term, an important word, or words that you see onscreen. For example, words in menus or dialog boxes appear in the text like this. Here is an example: "The **Model** stores the data required by the application according to commands sent by the Controller."

 Warnings or important notes appear like this.

 Tips and tricks appear like this.

Get in touch

Feedback from our readers is always welcome.

General feedback: Email feedback@packtpub.com and mention the book title in the subject of your message. If you have questions about any aspect of this book, please email us at questions@packtpub.com.

Errata: Although we have taken every care to ensure the accuracy of our content, mistakes do happen. If you have found a mistake in this book, we would be grateful if you would report this to us. Please visit www.packtpub.com/submit-errata, selecting your book, clicking on the Errata Submission Form link, and entering the details.

Piracy: If you come across any illegal copies of our works in any form on the Internet, we would be grateful if you would provide us with the location address or website name. Please contact us at copyright@packtpub.com with a link to the material.

If you are interested in becoming an author: If there is a topic that you have expertise in and you are interested in either writing or contributing to a book, please visit authors.packtpub.com.

Reviews

Please leave a review. Once you have read and used this book, why not leave a review on the site that you purchased it from? Potential readers can then see and use your unbiased opinion to make purchase decisions, we at Packt can understand what you think about our products, and our authors can see your feedback on their book. Thank you!

For more information about Packt, please visit packtpub.com.

1
TypeScript Best Practices

I've always hated JavaScript. I use it, sure, but only when necessary. I distinctly remember my first internship interview, back when I was a freshman at eXia.Cesi, a French computer engineering school. I only knew C and some Java, and I was asked to help on an intranet that mostly worked with homemade Ajax libraries. It was pure madness and kind of steered me away from the web aspect of computer engineering for a while. I find nothing likeable in the following:

```
var r = new XMLHttpRequest();
r.open("POST", "webservice", true);
r.onreadystatechange = function () {
    if (r.readyState != 4 || r.status != 200) return;
    console.log(r.responseText);
};
r.send("a=1&b=2&c=3");
```

A native Ajax call. How ugly is that?

Of course, with jQuery modules and some separation of concerns, it can be usable, but still not as comfortable as I would like. You can see in the following screenshot that the concerns are separated, but it's not so easy:

MathieuNls committed on **GitHub** Fix #167	
..	
MediaElement	file permissions
application.js	New click-based synchronization system #58
bootstrap.min.js	file permissions
facebook.js	file permissions
home.logic.js	Show only the resuts on the homepage #58
home.logic.mobile.js	file permissions
input.time.logic.js	Fix #167
jquery-ui.min.js	[WIP] Autocomplete brands and models
jquery.easy-autocomplete.min.js	add autocompletion real brand and models + pictures. #90
jquery.min.js	file permissions
jquery.min.map	file permissions
js.cookie.js	enable xss & csrf protections #144
rubytabs.js	Countdown for Atomic clock sync + accurate time everywhere
time.api.js	Countdown for Atomic clock sync + accurate time everywhere
time.js	Countdown for Atomic clock sync + accurate time everywhere
watch.animation.js	Countdown for Atomic clock sync + accurate time everywhere
watch.autocomplete.js	add autocompletion real brand and models + pictures. #90

A deprecated toolwatch.io version using PHP5 and Codeigniter

Then, I learned some RoR (a Ruby-based, object-oriented framework for web applications: `http://rubyonrails.org/`) and Hack (a typed PHP by Facebook: `http://hacklang.org/`). It was wonderful; I had everything I always wanted: type safety, tooling, and performance. The first one, type safety, is pretty self-explanatory:

```
<?hh
class MyClass {
  public function alpha(): int {
    return 1;
  }

  public function beta(): string {
    return 'hi test';
  }
}

function f(MyClass $my_inst): string {
  // Fix me!
  return $my_inst->alpha();
}
```

Also, with types, you can have great toolings, such as powerful auto completion and suggestions:

Sublime Text autocompletion on toolwatch.io mobile app (Ionic2 *[5]* + Angular 2)

Angular can be used with CoffeeScript, TypeScript, and JavaScript. In this book, we'll focus on TypeScript, which is the language recommended by Google. TypeScript is a typed superset of JavaScript; this means that, with TypeScript, you can do everything you used to do in JavaScript, and more! To name but a few advantages: user-defined types, inheritance, interfaces, and visibility. And the best part is that TypeScript is transpiled into JavaScript so that any modern browser can run it.

In fact, with the use of polyfill, even our good old IE6 can almost execute the final output. We'll get back to that in the next chapter. The transpilation is different from compilation (for example, from C to executable or `.java` to `.class`) as it only translates TypeScript into JavaScript.

In this chapter, we will learn the best practices for TypeScript. The syntax of the TypeScript language is quite easy to grasp for anyone who knows JavaScript and an object-oriented language. If you don't know anything about object-oriented programming, I'd suggest you put this book aside for a few moments and take a look at this quick Udacity course: `https://www.udacity.com/wiki/classes`.

As a summary of the topics covered:

- TypeScript syntax
- TypeScript best practices
- TypeScript shortcomings

Environment setup

For the environment setup, I will cover all three major platforms: Debian-flavored Linux, macOS, and Windows. All the tools we are going to use are cross-platform. Consequently, feel free to choose the one you like the most; there is not a thing you will not be able to do later on.

In what follows, we will install `Node.js`, npm, and TypeScript.

Node.js and npm for Linux

```
$ curl -sL https://deb.nodesource.com/setup_6.x | sudo -E bash -
$ sudo apt-get install -y Node.js
```

This command downloads a script, directly into your `bash`, that will fetch every resource you need and install it. For most cases, it will work just fine and install `Node.js` + npm.

Now, this script has one flaw; it will fail if you have Debian repositories that are no longer available. You can either take this opportunity to clean your Debian repositories or edit the script a bit.

```
$ curl https://deb.nodesource.com/setup_6.x > node.sh
$ sudo chmod +x node.sh
$ vim node.sh
//Comment out all apt-get update
//Save the file
$ sudo apt-get update
$ ./node.sh
$ sudo apt-get update
$ sudo apt-get install -y Node.js
```

Then, go to `https://Node.js.org/en/download/`, and download and install the last `.pkg` or `.msi` (for Linux or Windows, respectively).

TypeScript

Now, you should have access to `node` and `npm` in your Terminal. You can test them out with the following commands:

```
$ node -v
V8.9.0

$ npm -v
5.5.1
```

Note that the output of these commands (for example, v6.2.1 and 3.9.3) can be different, and your environment as the latest version of node and npm can, and most certainly, will be different by the time you read these lines. However, if you at least have these versions, you will be fine for the rest of this book:

```
$ npm install -g TypeScript
```

The `-g` argument stands for global. In the Linux system, depending on your distribution, you might need `sudo` rights to install global packages.

Very much like node and npm, we can test whether the installation went well with the following:

```
$ tsc -v
Version 2.6.1
```

What we have, for now, is the TypeScript transpiler. You can use it like so:

```
tsc --out myTranspiledFile.js myTypeScriptFile.ts
```

This command will transpile the content of `myTypeScriptFile.ts` and create `myTranspiledFile.js`. Then, you can execute the resultant `js` file, in the console, using node:

```
node myTranspiledFile.js
```

To speed up our development process, we will install `ts-node`. This node package will transpile TypeScript files into JavaScript and resolve the dependencies between said files:

```
$ npm install -g ts-node
$ ts-node -v
3.3.0
```

Create a file named `hello.ts` and add the following to it:

```
console.log('Hello World');
```

Now, we can use our new package:

```
$ ts-node hello.ts
Hello World
```

Quick overview

In this section, I'll present a quick overview of TypeScript. This presentation is by no means exhaustive, as I will explain particular concepts when we come across them. However, here are some basics.

TypeScript is, as I've mentioned, a typed superset of JavaScript. While TypeScript is typed, it only proposes four base types for you to use out of the box. The four types are `String`, `number`, `Boolean`, and `any`. These types can, using the : operator, type var name: string variables or function arguments and return the add(`a:number`, `b:number`):number type function. Also, `void` can be used for functions to specify that they don't return anything. On the object-oriented side, string, number, and boolean specialize any. `Any` can be used for anything. It's the TypeScript equivalent of the Java object.

If you need more than these types, well, you'll have to create them yourself! Thankfully, this is pretty straightforward. Here's the declaration of a user class that contains one property:

```
class Person{
name:String;
}
```

You can create a new `Person` instance with the simple command shown here:

```
var p:Person = new Person();
p.name = "Mathieu"
```

Here, I create a `p` variable that statically (for example, the left-hand side) and dynamically (for example, the right-hand side) stands for a Person. Then, I add `Mathieu` to the `name` property. Properties are, by default, public, but you can use the `public`, `private`, and `protected` keywords to refine their visibility. They'll behave as you'd expect in any object-oriented programming language.

TypeScript supports interfaces, inheritance, and polymorphism in a very simple fashion. Here is a simple hierarchy composed of two classes and one interface. The interface, `People`, defines the string that will be inherited by any `People` implementation. Then, `Employee` implements `People` and adds two properties: `manager` and `title`. Finally, the `Manager` class defines an `Employee` array, as shown in the following code block:

```
interface People{
    name:string;
}

class Employee implements People{
    manager:Manager;
    title:string;
}

class Manager extends Employee{
    team:Employee[];
}
```

Functions can be overridden by functions that have the same signature, and the `super` keyword can be used to refer to the parent implementation, as shown in the following snippet:

```
Interface People {

    name: string;
    presentSelf():void;
}

class Employee implements People {

    name: string;
    manager: Manager;
    title: string;
```

```
    presentSelf():void{

        console.log(

            "I am", this.name,
            ". My job is title and my boss is",
            this.manager.name

        );
    }
}


class Manager extends Employee {

    team: Employee[];

    presentSelf(): void {
        super.presentSelf();

        console.log("I also manage", this.team.toString());
    }
}
```

The last thing you need to know about TypeScript before we move on to the best practices is the difference between let and var. In TypeScript, you can use both to declare a variable.

Now, the particularity of variables in TypeScript is that it lets you decide between a function and a block scope for variables using the var and let keywords. Var will give your variable a function scope, while let will produce a block-scoped variable. A function scope means that the variables are visible and accessible to and from the whole function. Most programming languages have block scope for variables (such as C#, Java, and C++). Some languages also offer the same possibility as TypeScript, such as Swift 2. More concretely, the output of the following snippet will be 456:

```
var foo = 123;
if (true) {
    var foo = 456;
}
console.log(foo); // 456
```

In opposition, if you use let, the output will be `123` because the second `foo` variable only exists in the `if` block:

```
let foo = 123;
if (true) {
    let foo = 456;
}
console.log(foo); // 123
```

Best practices

In this section, we present the best practices for TypeScript in terms of coding conventions, tricks to use, and features and pitfalls to avoid.

Naming

The naming conventions preconized by the Angular and definitely typed teams are very simple:

- Class: `CamelCase`.
- Interface: `CamelCase`. Also, you should try to refrain from preceding your interface name with a capital I.
- Variables: `lowerCamelCase`. Private variables can be preceded by a _.
- Functions: `lowerCamelCase`. Also, if a method does not return anything, you should specify that said method returns `void` for better readability.

Interface redefinitions

TypeScript allows programmers to redefine interfaces, using the same name multiple times. Then, any implementation of said interface inherits all the definitions of all the interfaces. The official reason for this is to allow users to enhance the JavaScript interface without having to change the types of their object throughout their code. While I understand the intent of such a feature, I foresee way too much hassle in its use. Let's have a look at an example feature on the Microsoft website:

```
interface ICustomerMerge
{
    MiddleName: string;
}
```

```
interface ICustomerMerge
{
    Id: number;
}
class CustomerMerge implements ICustomerMerge
{
    id: number;
    MiddleName: string;
}
```

Leaving aside the fact that the naming conventions are not respected, we got two different definitions of the ICustomerMerge interface. The first one defines a string and the second one a number. Automatically, CustomerMerge has these members. Now, imagine you have ten-twelves file dependencies, you implement an interface, and you don't understand why you have to implement such and such functions. Well, someone, somewhere, decided it was pertinent to redefine an interface and broke all your code, at once.

Getters and setters

In TypeScript, you can specify optional arguments with the ? operator. While this feature is good and I will use it without moderation in the coming chapters, it opens the door to the following ugliness:

```
class User{
    private name:string;
    public  getSetName(name?:string):any{
        if(name !== undefined){
            this.name = name;
        }else{
            return this.name
        }
    }
}
```

Here, we test whether the optional name argument was passed with !== undefined. If the getSetName function received something, it'll act as a setter, otherwise, as a getter. The fact that the function doesn't return anything when used as a setter is authorized by any return type.

For clarity and readability, stick to the ActionScript-inspired getter and setter:

```
class User{
private name:_string = "Mathieu";
get name():String{
return this._name;
```

```
}
set name(name:String){
this._name = name;
}
}
```

Then, you can use them as follows:

```
var user:User = new User():
if(user.name === "Mathieu") { //getter
    user.name = "Paul" //setter
}
```

Constructor

TypeScript constructors offer a pretty unusual, but time-saving, feature. Indeed, they allow us to declare a class member directly. So, instead of this lengthy code:

```
class User{

    id:number;
    email:string;
    name:string;
    lastname:string;
    country:string;
    registerDate:string;
    key:string;


    constructor(id: number,email: string,name: string,
          lastname: string,country: string,registerDate:
          string,key: string){

          this.id = id;
          this.email = email;
          this.name = name;
          this.lastname = lastname;
          this.country = country;
          this.registerDate = registerDate;
          this.key = key;
    }
}
```

You could have:

```
class User{
    constructor(private id: number,private email: string,private name:
string,

          private lastname: string,private country: string, private
registerDate: string,private key: string){}
}
```

The preceding code achieves the same thing and will be transpiled to the same JavaScript. The only difference is that it saves you time in a way that doesn't degrade the clarity or readability of your code.

Type guards

Type guards, in TypeScript, define a list of types for a given value. If one of your variables can be assigned to one and only value or a specific set of values, then consider using the type guard over the enumerator. It'll achieve the same functionality while being much more concise. Here's a made-up example with a People person who has a gender attribute that can only be MALE or FEMALE:

```
class People{
gender: "male" | "female";
}
```

Now, consider the following:

```
class People{
gender:Gender;
}
enum Gender{
MALE, FEMALE
}
```

Enumerator

In opposition to type guards, if your class has a variable that can take multiple values at the same time from a finite list of values, then consider using the bit-based enumerator. Here's an excellent example from https://basarat.gitbooks.io/:

```
class Animal{
    flags:AnimalFlags = AnimalFlags.None
}
```

```
enum AnimalFlags {
    None            = 0,
    HasClaws        = 1 << 0,
    CanFly          = 1 << 1,
}

function printAnimalAbilities(animal) {
    var animalFlags = animal.flags;
    if (animalFlags & AnimalFlags.HasClaws) {
        console.log('animal has claws');
    }
    if (animalFlags & AnimalFlags.CanFly) {
        console.log('animal can fly');
    }
    if (animalFlags == AnimalFlags.None) {
        console.log('nothing');
    }
}

var animal = { flags: AnimalFlags.None };
printAnimalAbilities(animal); // nothing
animal.flags |= AnimalFlags.HasClaws;
printAnimalAbilities(animal); // animal has claws
animal.flags &= ~AnimalFlags.HasClaws;
printAnimalAbilities(animal); // nothing
animal.flags |= AnimalFlags.HasClaws | AnimalFlags.CanFly;
printAnimalAbilities(animal); // animal has claws, animal can fly
```

We defined the different values using the << shift operator in `AnimalFlags`, then used `|=` to combine flags, `&=` and `~` to remove flags, and `|` to combine flags.

Pitfalls

In this section, we will go over two TypeScript pitfalls that became a problem for me when I was coding Angular 2 applications.

Type-casting and JSON

If you plan to build more than a playground with Angular 2, and you obviously do since you are interested in patterns for performances, stability, and operations, you will most likely consume an API to feed your application. Chances are, this API will communicate with you using JSON.

Let's assume that we have a `User` class with two private variables: `lastName:string` and `firstName:string`. In addition, this simple class proposes the `hello` method, which prints `Hi I am`, `this.firstName`, `this.lastName`:

```
class User{
    constructor(private lastName:string,         private firstName:string){
    }

    hello(){
        console.log("Hi I am", this.firstName,          this.lastName);
    }
}
```

Now, consider that we receive users through a JSON API. Most likely, it'll look something like `[{"lastName":"Nayrolles","firstName":"Mathieu"}...]`. With the following snippet, we can create a `User`:

```
let userFromJSONAPI: User =
JSON.parse('[{"lastName":"Nayrolles","firstName":"Mathieu"}]')[0];
```

So far, the TypeScript compiler doesn't complain, and it executes smoothly. It works because the `parse` method returns `any` (that is, the TypeScript equivalent of the Java object). Sure enough, we can convert `any` into `User`. However, the following `userFromJSONAPI.hello();` will yield:

```
json.ts:19
userFromJSONAPI.hello();
                 ^

TypeError: userFromUJSONAPI.hello is not a function
    at Object.<anonymous> (json.ts:19:18)
    at Module._compile (module.js:541:32)
    at Object.loader (/usr/lib/node_modules/ts-node/src/ts-
node.ts:225:14)
    at Module.load (module.js:458:32)
    at tryModuleLoad (module.js:417:12)
    at Function.Module._load (module.js:409:3)
    at Function.Module.runMain (module.js:575:10)
    at Object.<anonymous> (/usr/lib/node_modules/ts-node/src/bin/ts-
node.ts:110:12)
    at Module._compile (module.js:541:32)
    at Object.Module._extensions..js (module.js:550:10)
```

Why? Well, the left-hand side of the assignation is defined as User, sure, but it'll be *erased* when we transpile it to JavaScript. The type-safe TypeScript way to do it is:

```
let validUser =
JSON.parse('[{"lastName":"Nayrolles","firstName":"Mathieu"}]')
.map((json: any):User => {
return new User(json.lastName, json.firstName);
})[0];
```

Interestingly enough, the typeof function won't help you either. In both cases, it'll display Object instead of User, as the very concept of User doesn't exist in JavaScript.

This type of fetch/map/new can rapidly become tedious as the parameter list grows. You can use the factory pattern which we'll see in Chapter 3, *Classical Patterns*, or create an instance loader, such as:

```
class InstanceLoader {
    static getInstance<T>(context: Object, name: string, rawJson:any): T {
        var instance:T = Object.create(context[name].prototype);
        for(var attr in instance){
         instance[attr] = rawJson[attr];
         console.log(attr);
        }
        return <T>instance;
    }
}
InstanceLoader.getInstance<User>(this, 'User',
JSON.parse('[{"lastName":"Nayrolles","firstName":"Mathieu"}]')[0])
```

InstanceLoader will only work when used inside an HTML page, as it depends on the window variable. If you try to execute it using ts-node, you'll get the following error:

```
ReferenceError: window is not defined
```

Inheritance and polymorphism

Let's assume that we have a simple inheritance hierarchy as follows. We have an interface Animal that defines the eat():void and sleep(): void methods:

```
interface Animal{ eat():void; sleep():void; }
```

Then, we have a `Mammal` class that implements the `Animal` interface. This class also adds a constructor and leverages the private `name: type` notation we saw earlier. For the `eat():void` and `sleep(): void` methods, this class prints `"Like a mammal"`:

```
class Mammal implements Animal{

    constructor(private name:string){
        console.log(this.name, "is alive");
    }

    eat(){
        console.log("Like a mammal");
    }

    sleep(){
        console.log("Like a mammal");
    }
}
```

We also have a `Dog` class that extends `Mammal` and overrides `eat(): void` so it prints `"Like a Dog"`:

```
class Dog extends Mammal{
    eat(){
        console.log("Like a dog")
    }
}
```

Finally, we have a function that expects an `Animal` as a parameter and invokes the `eat()` method:

```
let mammal: Mammal = new Mammal("Mammal");
let dolly: Dog = new Dog("Dolly");
let prisca: Mammal = new Dog("Prisca");
let abomination: Dog = new Mammal("abomination"); //-> Wait. WHAT ?!
function makeThemEat (animal:Animal):void{
    animal.eat();
}
```

The output is as follows:

```
ts-node class-inheritance-polymorhism.ts
Mammal is alive

Dolly is alive
Prisca is alive
abomination is alive
Like a mammal
Like a dog
Like a dog
Like a mammal
```

Now, our last creation, `let abomination: Dog = new Mammal("abomination");` should not be possible as per object-oriented principles. Indeed, the left-hand side of the affectation is more specific than the right-hand side, which should not be allowed by the TypeScript compiler. If we look at the generated JavaScript, we can see what happens. The types disappear and are replaced by functions. Then, the types of the variables are inferred at creation time:

```
var __extends = (this && this.__extends) || function (d, b) {
    for (var p in b) if (b.hasOwnProperty(p)) d[p] = b[p];
    function __() { this.constructor = d; }
    d.prototype = b === null ? Object.create(b) : (__.prototype =
b.prototype, new __());
};
var Mammal = (function () {
    function Mammal() {
    }
    Mammal.prototype.eat = function () {
        console.log("Like a mammal");
    };
    Mammal.prototype.sleep = function () {
        console.log("Like a mammal");
    };
    return Mammal;
}());
var Dog = (function (_super) {
    __extends(Dog, _super);
    function Dog() {
        _super.apply(this, arguments);
    }
    Dog.prototype.eat = function () {
        console.log("Like a dog");
    };
    return Dog;
}(Mammal));
```

```
function makeThemEat(animal) {
    animal.eat();
}
var mammal = new Mammal();
var dog = new Dog();
var labrador = new Mammal();
makeThemEat(mammal);
makeThemEat(dog);
makeThemEat(labrador);
```

 When in doubt, it's always a good idea to look at the transpiled JavaScript. You will see what's going on at execution time and maybe discover other pitfalls! As a side note, the TypeScript transpiler is fooled here because, from a JavaScript point of view, Mammal and Dog are not different; they have the same properties and functions. If we add a property in the Dog class (such as private race:string), it won't transpile anymore. This means that overriding methods are not sufficient to be recognized as types; they must be semantically different.

This example is a bit far-fetched, and I agree that this TypeScript specificity won't haunt you every day. However, if we are using some bounded genericity with a strict hierarchy, then you have to know about it. Indeed, the following example, unfortunately, works:

```
function makeThemEat<T extends Dog>(dog:T):void{
    dog.eat();
}

makeThemEat<Mammal>(abomination);
```

Summary

In this chapter, we completed a TypeScript setup and reviewed most of the best practices in terms of code convention, features we should and shouldn't use, and common pitfalls to avoid.

In the next chapter, we will focus on Angular and how to get started with the all-new Angular CLI.

Angular Bootstrapping

2

After `Chapter 1`, *Typescript Best Practices*, we can dive into Angular itself. One of the focuses of Angular was to drastically improve the performance and loading time of Angular applications compared to AngularJS. The performance improvements are outstanding. According to the Angular team and various benchmarks, Angular 2 is between five and eight times faster than Angular 1.

Now, to achieve this kind of improvement, Google engineers did not build upon AngularJS; instead, they created Angular from scratch. Consequently, having worked with Angular 1 for some time, this will not give you a sizable edge over newcomers to the Angular world when it comes to developing Angular applications.

In this chapter, we will do the following:

- I will first present the major architectural concepts behind Angular.
- Then, we will bootstrap an Angular application using the newly introduced Angular CLI tool that takes away most of the getting started pain. There are hundreds of Angular boilerplates on the web, and choosing one can be time-consuming, to say the least. You can enjoy any flavors on GitHub with tests, with libraries, for mobiles, with build and deployment scripts, and so on.

While this diversity and enthusiasm from the community is a good thing, it means that no two Angular projects look the same. Indeed, the chances are that both projects were created with a different boilerplate or without any. To fix this problem, the Angular team is now proposing angular CLI. Angular CLI is a command-line node package that allows developers to create new applications based on an official boilerplate. This tool also provides some useful features, such as the creation of the different building blocks of an Angular application, building, testing, and minifying your application. It even supports the deployment of your application to GitHub pages with one short command.

It's still a new tool, and it has numerous drawbacks and unpolished behaviors.

Architectural overview

In this section, I will present the main building blocks of Angular applications: **Service**, **Component**, **Template**, and **Directive**. We will also learn what problems are solved by dependency injection, decorators, and zones.

Now, if you picked this book off the (virtual) shelf, you likely have some experience with Angular and want to improve your applications with good practices and design patterns. Therefore, you should have some knowledge about the general architecture of Angular building blocks.

Nevertheless, a quick and pragmatic reminder should not hurt much, and we can be sure that we have a solid architectural basis to build our patterns upon.

Here is an overview of how the main Angular 2 building blocks interact with each other:

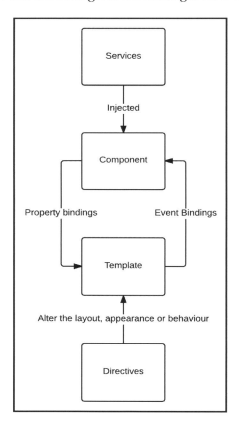

High-level architecture of an Angular 2 application

In what follows, I will present an example of each Angular 2 building block by creating an application that manipulates the Floyd array. Here is an example of a letter-based Floyd array:

```
a
b c
d e f
g h i j
```

I agree that you are not very likely to build an application dealing with Floyd arrays in the near future. Nevertheless, Floyd arrays are a good programming exercise when learning a new language or framework, as it involves user input, displaying results, loops, and string manipulation.

Component

Components are the views of our Angular application in the sense that they control what, when, and how things should be displayed on the screen. They take the form of a simple class that defines the logic required by your views. Here's an example of a simple component:

```
export class FloydComponent implements OnInit {

  private floydString:string = "";
  private static startOfAlphabet = 97;

  constructor() { }

  ngOnInit() {
  }

  onClick(rows:number){
    let currentLetter = FloydComponent.startOfAlphabet;
    for (let i = 0; i < rows; i++) {
      for (let j = 0; j < i; j++) {
        this.floydString += String.fromCharCode(currentLetter) + " ";
        currentLetter++;
      }
      this.floydString += "\n\r";
    }
  }
}
```

Note that the component class has a suffix: `Component`. I will discuss the reasons in the next chapter.

This component named `FloydComponent` has two private members: `floydString` and `startOfAlphabet`. The `floydString` will contain the string representing an nth Floyd triangle, while `startOfAlphabet` is constantly marking the position of the letter in the ASCII table.

The `FloydComponent` also defines a constructor, which will be invoked when the user requests the patch of screen our component manages. For now, the constructor is empty.

Finally, the `onClick` method accepting a number argument called `rows` will generate a Floyd triangle of `rows`. To sum up, we have a class managing the behavior of a view showcasing a Floyd triangle. Yes? Well, the view part is kind of missing! Where is my HTML for client-side rendering?

In Angular, the piece of HTML our component will have control over is known as a template, and we can link the template on the component using metadata:

```typescript
import { Component } from '@angular/core';
@Component({
  selector: 'floyd',
  template:
  `<p>
    <input #checkbox type="checkbox" value="even">Even?<br>
    <input #rows type="text" name="rows">
    <button (click)="onClick(rows.value, checkbox.checked)">CLICK</button>
  </p>
  <pre>
        {{floydString}}
  </pre>
  `
})
export class FloydComponent {
```

So, what's all that fuss about? If we look back at the original definition of the `FloydComponent`, there's nothing specifying that `FloydComponent` is a component. We don't have anything like `FloydComponent` extending/implementing components, so it's just a plain typescript class and nothing else. Even more surprisingly, there are no Angular references at all; this `FloydComponent` could totally be a typescript class outside of the Angular framework.

The metadata is decorating the `FloydComponent` class using the decorator pattern, so Angular knows how to interpret and process the `FloydComponent` class.

 In any object-oriented languages, it is easy to extend the responsibilities of an object statically by using inheritance, however, doing so dynamically, at runtime, is a completely different matter. The purpose of the decorator pattern is to add additional responsibilities dynamically to an object.

We will implement our very own decorator in `Chapter 3`, *Classical Patterns*.

The annotation itself is `@Component`, and makes our class an Angular component with some arguments.

 Note the `import { Component } from '@angular/core';` which imports the `Component` module from the `'@angular/core'` library.

The first argument is a `selector` that describes which part of the view our `FloydComponent` should bind itself to. In the following HTML snippet, we have the `<floyd></floyd>` selector markup that the `FloydComponent` will bind to. The second argument is the template string. The template string defines what will be added to the DOM, at runtime, inside the `<floyd>` markup:

```
<p>
  <input #rows type="text" name="rows">
  <button (click)="onClick(rows.value)">CLICK</button>
</p>
<pre>
      {{floydString}}
</pre>
```

 The backtick ` allows us to define multiline strings in JavaScript.

First, we have the `<input>` markup, which looks almost like pure HTML. The only particularity is the `#rows` attribute in the markup. This attribute is used to reference the markup as a variable named `rows`. Hence, we can access its value in the following markup: `<button (click)="onClick(rows.value)">CLICK</button>`. Here, we have an event binding between the template and the component. When the button is clicked, the `onClick` method of the component will be invoked, and the value of the input will be fed to the method.

Further down the code, we have `{{floydString}}`, which is a property binding from the component to the template. In this particular case, we bind the `floydString` component property to the template. In other words, we display the content of the `floydString` component property in the DOM.

> I have to use the pre markup, so the `\n\r` are preserved in the output.

To sum this up, the component binds its property to the template and the template binds its events to the component. Here's a screenshot of what to expect when running this application:

Floyd array with Angular 2

> Is it not working on your side? Want to fork the code on GitHub? You can see the whole application, as of now, at `http://bit.ly/angular2-patterns-chap2`.

Services

For now, we have reviewed two out of four of the building blocks of Angular 2. The remaining two are services and directives. The next block we are going to review services. Services are classes with a unique purpose that shall be, as much as possible, cohesive in the sense that they provide a narrow and well-defined service to other parts of the application. From a design point of view, what could be nice for our Floyd triangle application is to have the content of the `FloydComponent.onClick` method inside a service. Indeed, the computation of the `floydString` string does not have its place in a component managing the view.

A component should only be in charge of the user experience—binding properties to a template—and nothing else. Every other one should be delegated to services. What we can do is create a triangle service that will be in charge of *drum rolls* creating weird triangles such as Floyd triangle. We can also make this service in charge of generating Floyd triangles where the output would be looking like a tree:

```
    a
   b c
  d e f
 g h i j
```

Instead of:

```
a
b c
d e f
g h i j
```

Such a service would look like the following:

```
import { Injectable } from '@angular/core';

@Injectable()
export class TriangleService {
    private static startOfAlphabet = 97;
    constructor() {}
    /**
     * Computes a Floyd Triangle of letter.
     * Here's an example for rows = 5
     *
     * a
     * b c
     * d e f
     * g h i j
     *
     * Adapted from
http://www.programmingsimplified.com/c-program-print-floyd-triangle
     *
     * @param  {number} rows
     * @return {string}
     */
    public floydTriangle(rows:number):string{
      let currentLetter = TriangleService.startOfAlphabet;
      let resultString = "";
      for (let i = 0; i < rows; i++) {
        for (let j = 0; j < i; j++) {
          resultString += String.fromCharCode(currentLetter) + " ";
          currentLetter++;
```

```
      }
      resultString += "\n\r";
    }
    return resultString;
  }
  /**
   * Computes a Even Floyd Triangle of letter.
   * Here's an example for rows = 7
   *        a
   *       b c
   *      d e f
   *     g h i j
   *    k l m n o
   *   p q r s t u
   * v w x y z { |
   *
   * @param   {number} rows
   * @return {string}
   */
  public evenFloydTriangle(rows:number):string{
    let currentLetter = TriangleService.startOfAlphabet;
    let resultString = "";
    for (let i = 0; i < rows; i++) {
      for (let j = 0; j <= (rows-i-2); j++) {
        resultString += " ";
      }
      for (let j = 0; j <= i; j++) {
        resultString += String.fromCharCode(currentLetter) + " ";
        currentLetter++;
      }
      resultString+="\n\r";
    }
    return resultString;
  }
}
```

The `TriangleService` is a simple class that offers two methods: `floydTriangle` and `evenFloydTriangle`. The `evenFloydTriangle` has an additional for loop to add the leading spaces at the different rows of the triangle. The business application now sits on a dedicated service that we can use on our `FloydComponent`. The right way to use our service in the `FloydComponent` is through dependency injection. Dependency injection is a process by which a requesting class gets a fully formed instance of a requested class dynamically. To apply this rather technical definition to our context, upon instantiation, the `FloydComponent` will be served an instance of the `TriangleService`.

To use dependency injection with Angular, we need to define a provider for the TriangleService. We can do this at the application level:

```
import { TriangleService } from './app/triangle.service'

bootstrap(FloydComponent, [TriangleService]);
```

Alternatively, we can do this at the component level by defining providers in the component annotations:

```
import { Component, OnInit, ViewEncapsulation } from '@angular/core';
import { TriangleService } from '../triangle.service'

@Component({
  selector: 'floyd',
  template:    `<p>
    <input #checkbox type="checkbox" value="even">Even?<br>
  <input #rows type="text" name="rows">
  <button (click)="onClick(rows.value, checkbox.checked)">CLICK</button>
  </p>
  <pre>

  {{floydString}}
  </pre>
  `,
  styleUrls: ['./floyd.component.css'],
  providers: [TriangleService],
  encapsulation: ViewEncapsulation.None
})
export class FloydComponent implements OnInit {
```

If the provider is created at the application level, then the same instance of the TriangleService will be served to anyone requesting it. At the component level, however, a new instance of the TriangleService will be created and served to the component each time said component is instantiated. Both cases can make sense. It depends on what your components and your services are doing. For example, the logging service we will implement in Chapter 7, *Operations Patterns*, does not have a state of its own and is used by every module of the application. Consequently, we can use an application-based provider. The counterexample would be the *Circuit breaker* pattern from Chapter 5, *Stability Patterns*, which does have an inner state, and hence, a component level.

The final touch is to modify our `FloydComponent` constructor so that it looks like this:

```
constructor(private triangleService:TriangleService) {
}
```

Here, we define a private member named `triangleService` for our `FloydComponent`, which will be used as a placeholder for the injected dependency.

In addition, we add a checkbox in the template, which will be used to determine if we want an even or a normal Floyd array:

```
<input #rows type="text" name="rows">
  <button (click)="onClick(rows.value, checkbox.checked)">CLICK</button>
```

We can also modify the `onClick` method to use our `TriangleService`. The final component looks like this:

```
import { Component, OnInit, ViewEncapsulation } from '@angular/core';
import { TriangleService } from '../triangle.service'

@Component({
  selector: 'floyd',
  template:    `<p>
    <input #checkbox type="checkbox" value="even">Even?<br>
  <input #rows type="text" name="rows">
  <button (click)="onClick(rows.value, checkbox.checked)">CLICK</button>
  </p>
  <pre>
    {{floydString}}
  </pre>
  `,
  styleUrls: ['./floyd.component.css'],
  providers: [TriangleService],
  encapsulation: ViewEncapsulation.None
})
export class FloydComponent implements OnInit {

  private floydString:string = "";
  private static startOfAlphabet = 97;

  constructor(private triangleService:TriangleService) { }

  ngOnInit() {
  }

  onClick(rows:number, checked:boolean){
```

```
    if(checked){
      this.floydString = this.triangleService.evenFloydTriangle(rows);
    }else{
      this.floydString = this.triangleService.floydTriangle(rows);
    }
  }
}
```

The current state of the application can be seen here: `http://bit.ly/angular2-patterns-chap2-part2`.

Directives

To conclude our quick architectural overview, we will create a directive to enhance our rather fade pre-markup. Directives are interacting with a template and with their parent component regarding property and event bindings. We will create a directive that adds style to our pre-markup. The style involves a 1 px border and changes the background color to red or yellow for an even or odd Floyd array, respectively.

First, we need a way to ask the user which kind of array he/she wants. Let's add another input in the template of the `FloydComponent` and modify the `onClick` method so it accepts a second argument:

```
import { Component } from '@angular/core';
import { TriangleService } from '../triangle.service';
@Component({
  selector: 'floyd',
  template:
  `<p>
    <input #checkbox type="checkbox" value="even">Even?<br>
    <input #rows type="text" name="rows">
    <button (click)="onClick(rows.value, checkbox.checked)">CLICK</button>
  </p>
  <pre>
        {{floydString}}
  </pre>
  `,
  providers:    [TriangleService]
})
export class FloydComponent {

  private floydString:string = "";
```

```
private color:"yellow" | "red";

constructor(private triangleService:TriangleService) {

}

onClick(rows:number, even:boolean){

  if(even){
        this.floydString = this.triangleService.evenFloydTriangle(rows);
  }else{
        this.floydString = this.triangleService.floydTriangle(rows);
  }

}

}
```

Then, we can create the directive. It will look like the following:

```
import { Directive, Input, ElementRef, HostListener } from '@angular/core';

@Directive({
  selector: '[AngularPre]'
})
export class AngularPre {

  @Input()
  highlightColor:string;


  constructor(private el: ElementRef) {
      el.nativeElement.style.border = "1px solid black";
       el.nativeElement.style.backgroundColor = this.highlightColor;
  }

    @HostListener('mouseenter') onMouseEnter() {
        this.highlight(this.highlightColor);
  }
  @HostListener('mouseleave') onMouseLeave() {
      this.highlight(null);
  }

  private highlight(color: string) {
        this.el.nativeElement.style.backgroundColor = color;
  }

}
```

A lot happens here. First, we have the directive annotation with a selector. The selector will be used to signify that a given HTML markup depends on the directive. In our case, I chose to name the directive AngularPre and to have the same name for the selector. They can be different; it is up to you. However, it does make sense to have the same name for the selector and the class so you know which file to open when your directive is going sideways.

Then, we have the very interesting @Input() annotating the highlightColor:string; member. Here, we specify that the value of the highlightColor string is, in fact, bound to the variable from the parent component. In other words, the parent will have to specify the color in which it wants the pre-markup to be highlighted. In the constructor, the directive received an ElementRef object by injection. This ElementRef represents the DOM on which your directive acts. Finally, we define two HostListener on mouseenter and mouseleave that will start and stop the highlighting of the pre-markup, respectively.

To use this directive, we have to insert its selector in the pre-markup of the FloydComponent template as follows:

```
<pre AngularPre [highlightColor]="color">
    {{floydString}}
</pre>
```

Here, we specify that we want our pre-markup to be affected by the directive with the AngularPre selector, and we bind the highlightColor variable of the invoked directive with the color variable of the FloydComponent. Here's the FloydComponent with the color variable and a slight modification of the onClick method, so it changes the value of the color variable:

```
export class FloydComponent {

  private floydString:string = "";
  private color:"yellow" | "red";

  constructor(private triangleService:TriangleService) {

  }

  onClick(rows:number, even:boolean){

   if(even){
        this.floydString = this.triangleService.evenFloydTriangle(rows);
        this.color = "red";
   }else{
        this.floydString = this.triangleService.floydTriangle(rows);
```

```
        this.color = "yellow";
    }

  }

}
onClick modifies the color variable
```

This is what the application looks like with an odd array:

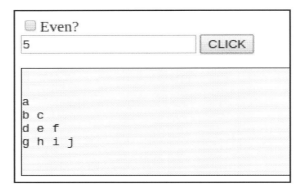

Odd Floyd array result

This is what it looks like with an even array:

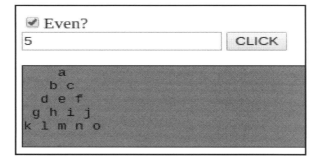

Even Floyd array result

The application is downloadable here: `http://bit.ly/angular2-patterns-chap2-part3.`

Pipes

The last two building blocks that I want to explain here are pipes and routes. pipes are wonderful. They allow us to create a specialized class that will take and transform any input into the desired output. In Angular, pipes follow the Unix pipes programming paradigm, where information can be passed from one process to another. What we can do with our Floyd triangle-based application creates a Pipe that will transform any given Floyd string to include the ASCII character for a paragraph ¶ (244, `&para;`) every time it encounters the newline sequences (such as \n\r):

```
import { Pipe, PipeTransform } from '@angular/core';

@Pipe({
  name: 'paragraph'
})
export class ParagraphPipe implements PipeTransform {

  transform(value: string): string {

    return value.replace(
        new RegExp("\n\r", 'g'),
        "¶ \n\r"
    );
  }

}
```

Pipes are decorated using the `@Pipe` annotation very much like component and directive. Now, the difference with pipes, compared to component and directive, is that, as well as decorating the annotation, we have to implement an interface provided by the Angular framework. This interface is named `PipeTransform` and defines a single method that every class implementing it must have:

```
transform(value: any, args?:any): any
```

The actual signature of this method is composed of any types, as pipes can be used for everything, not only strings. In our case, we want to manipulate a string input and have a string output. We can refine the signature of the transform method without breaking the interface contract, as follows:

```
transform(value: string): string
```

Here, we expect only one string argument and produce a string output. The body of this method contains a global regex matching all the \n\r sequence and adds ¶.

To use the `ParagraphPipe` in the `FloydComponent`, we have to modify the template as follows:

```
`<p>

  <input #checkbox type="checkbox" value="even">Even?<br>

  <input #rows type="text" name="rows">

  <button (click)="onClick(rows.value, checkbox.checked)">CLICK</button>

</p>

<pre AngularPre [highlightColor]="color">


      {{floydString | paragraph}}

</pre>
```

The `floydString` is piped to the `ParagraphPipe` using the | operator. Here's what's it looks like:

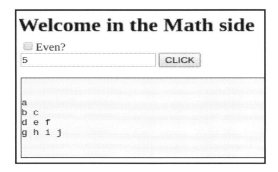

Piping the floydString to have a paragraph marker

The fact that the paragraph pipe hardcodes the paragraph symbol bugs me a little. What if I want to change it on a per-usage basis? Well, Angular is handling many additional parameters for your pipes. We can modify the transform method to the following:

```
transform(value: string, paragrapheSymbol:string): string {

    return value.replace(

        new RegExp("\n\r", 'g'),

        paragrapheSymbol + "\n\r"

    );

}
```

Moreover, we can do so with the pipe call like so:

```
{{floydString | paragraph: "¶"}}
```

Here, the first argument of the transform method will be the floydString, while the second will be the paragraph symbol.

If we think about it, we are currently implementing the replaceAll function for Typescript except for the target (\n\r is hardcoded). Let's create a Pipe named replaceAll that has both the target to replace and its replacement as a parameter. The only problem is that the PipeTransform interface defines a transform method with two parameters, the second one being optional. Here, we need three parameters: the string to transform, the target to replace inside the string, and the replacement for the target. If you do try to have a transform method with three parameters, then you will break the PipeTransform contract, and your Typescript will not compile anymore. To circumvent this minor setback, we can define an inline type named replace that will contain two members, from and to, that are both strings:

```
transform(value: string, replace: {from:string, to:string}): string
To call it inside the FloydComponent we can do the following:

{{floydString | replaceAll: {from:'\\n\\r', to:'¶ \\n\\r'} }}
```

Here, we are using `\\n\\r` for the strings pattern as we are not building a RegExp just yet. Consequently, the `\` of `\n` and `\r` need to be escaped.

Here's the code of the `replaceAll` pipe:

```
import { Pipe, PipeTransform } from '@angular/core';

@Pipe({
  name: 'replaceAll'
})
export class ReplaceAllPipe implements PipeTransform {

  transform(value: string, replace: {from:string, to:string}): string {

    return value.replace(
          new RegExp(replace.from, 'g'),
          replace.to
    );

  }

}
```

Not so bad, huh? We have filled one of the shortcomings of JavaScript, the `replaceAll` functionality, in a modular and efficient way. This `replaceAll` pipe will be usable everywhere in your application:

```
@Component({
  selector: 'floyd',
  template:    `<p>
    <input #checkbox type="checkbox" value="even">Even?<br>
  <input #rows type="text" name="rows">
  <button (click)="onClick(rows.value, checkbox.checked)">CLICK</button>
  </p>
  <pre AngularPre [highlightColor]="color">
    {{floydString | replaceAll: {from:'\\n\\r', to:'¶ \\n\\r'} }}
  </pre>
  `,
  styleUrls: ['./floyd.component.css'],
  providers: [TriangleService],
  encapsulation: ViewEncapsulation.None
})
export class FloydComponent implements OnInit {
```

The last thing to know about the pipes is that you can combine them just like in the Unix console. For example, we could totally do the following, where the paragraph pipe kicks in first and adds the ¶ to the end of all lines. Then, the `replaceAll` pipe intervenes and replaces all the ¶ by ¶ piped:

```
{{floydString | paragraph:'¶' | replaceAll: {from:'¶', to:'¶ piped'} }}
```

The current state of the application is downloadable here: `http://bit.ly/angular2-patterns-chap2-part5`.

Routes

Routes enable navigation between Angular views. In this recipe, we'll learn about them and see them in action within the framework of a small application.

Angular CLI

The **Angular CLI** is a very simple, yet extremely useful, node package that takes the form of a command-line tool. The purpose of this tool is to take away most of the pain of getting started with Angular 2. The problem with any application based on a framework is to know how to bootstrap things for your code to communicate smoothly with the framework's features and libraries.

This tool, provided directly by the Angular team, provides working blueprints for ready-to-go applications. Indeed, by using one simple command we can generate a complete boilerplate for Angular that can be transpiled, run locally, tested, and even deployed to GitHub pages.

Installation

Installing the Angular CLI is dead simple as it's a `node` package. The following command will work, regardless of your operating system:

```
npm install -g angular-cli
```

If you are using a Unix-based system, a `sudo` might be required for global installations.

Creating a new application

Once the Angular CLI is installed, we can begin by generating a new Angular application with the `ng new` command:

```
ng new MyApp
```

This command will create an empty boilerplate for your application and fetch every required node module.

Note that, depending on your internet connection, this command can take a while to complete. Indeed, the node packages to fetch are many, which further justifies such a tool.

At the root level of the newly created folder, you can find the following files and folders:

- `Angular-cli-build.js`: A config file to build your application.
- `config`: A config folder for the test environment.
- `Node_modules`: The different node modules required. As I am writing these lines, the current version of the Angular CLI already has 60,886 files and folders in the node-modules directory.
- `Public`: Contains what's public for your app.
- `tslint.json`: Configuration for your linter. We will configure it in the next chapter.
- `typings.json`: Typings dependencies.
- `angular-cli.json`: Some configuration for your app.
- `e2e`: e2e configuration.
- `package.json`: Dependencies for your app.
- `src`: Your source code.
- `typings`: Required typings.

Indisputably, the folder in which we will spend the most time is the src folder, as it contains the TypeScript source code. Here's what's inside it after creation:

```
src

├─── app

│      ├─── environment.ts

│      ├─── index.ts

│      ├─── my-app.component.css

│      ├─── my-app.component.html

│      ├─── my-app.component.spec.ts

│      ├─── my-app.component.ts

│      └─── shared

│              └─── index.ts

├─── favicon.ico

├─── index.html

├─── main.ts

├─── system-config.ts
```

```
├────  tsconfig.json


└────  typings.d.ts
```

As you can see, there is an `app` folder that already contains a component named `my-app` and a shared folder that can be used to share resources between different apps. Then, we have the `index.html` containing the following:

```
<!doctype html>
<html lang="en">
<head>
  <meta charset="utf-8">
  <title>Chap2</title>
  <base href="/">

  <meta name="viewport" content="width=device-width, initial-scale=1">
  <link rel="icon" type="image/x-icon" href="favicon.ico">
</head>
<body>
  <app-root></app-root>
</body>
</html>
```

In this `index.html`, the `<app-root></app-root>` markup is inserted and the required files are loaded into the script.

Another important point is the `main.ts` file, which contains the bootstrapping lines for your application:

```
import { enableProdMode } from '@angular/core';
import { platformBrowserDynamic } from '@angular/platform-browser-dynamic';

import { AppModule } from './app/app.module';
import { environment } from './environments/environment';

if (environment.production) {
  enableProdMode();
}

platformBrowserDynamic().bootstrapModule(AppModule)
  .catch(err => console.log(err));
```

Here, the `MyAppAppComponent` component is imported and used as the top-level or root component for our application. This is the component that will be instantiated first.

Generating

For now, our application is not exactly exciting; it will only display `my-app works!` in an h1 markup.

If we want to add components, directives, services, and pipes to this boilerplate, we have to use the `generate` command. Here's an example to generate a new component named `Floyd`:

ng generate component Floyd

In response, the Angular CLI created a new folder named `Floyd` and the required files for our component:

```
src/app

├── environment.ts

├── Floyd

│   ├── floyd.component.css

│   ├── floyd.component.html

│   ├── floyd.component.spec.ts

│   ├── floyd.component.ts

│   └── index.ts

├── index.ts

├── my-app.component.css

├── my-app.component.html
```

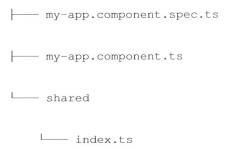

```
├── my-app.component.spec.ts

├── my-app.component.ts

└── shared

    └── index.ts
```

We can do the same operation using directive, service, or pipe instead of component.

> Every keyword in the Angular CLI can be abbreviated by using only the first letter of the word. So, generating another component named `Pascal` would read `ng g c Pascal`.

Serving

We have a bunch of components, services, directives, and pipes in our application, and we are ready to see the result. Thankfully, Angular CLI can build your application and start up a web server using the command `ng serve`.

Then, you can see your application at `localhost:4200`.

Your files are watched by the Angular CLI. Every time you make a change to a file, the Angular CLI will recompile it and refresh your browser.

Deploying

Ready to make your application live? `ng build` is what you are looking for. This command will create a `dist` directory that you can push onto any server capable of serving HTML pages. It can even be on GitHub pages, which will not cost you a single cent.

Summary

In this chapter, we have completed an overview of the Angular building blocks and seen how they interact with each other. We have also created a relatively simple application manipulating Floyd arrays. Finally, we learned how to use the Angular CLI to create new applications, components, services, directives, and pipes using the command line.

In the next chapter, we will focus on Angular good practices. We will discover the "do's and don'ts" recommended by Google engineers in a practical way.

3
Classical Patterns

TypeScript is an object-oriented programming language and, as such, we can leverage decades of knowledge on object-oriented architecture. In this chapter, we'll explore some of the most useful object-oriented design patterns and learn how to apply them in an Angular way.

Angular is, by itself, an object-oriented framework, and it forces you to do most of your development in certain ways. For example, you are required to have components, services, pipes, and so on. Forcing these building blocks upon you contributes to building a good architecture, very much like what the Zend framework does for PHP, or Ruby on Rails for Ruby. Of course, frameworks are there to make your life easier and speed up development time.

While the Angular way of designing things is way above average, we can always do better. I do not claim that what I present in this chapter is the ultimate design, or that you will be able to use it to resolve anything from bakery one-pagers to dashboards for the Mars One mission—such a design doesn't exist, unfortunately—but it'll definitively improve your toolbelt.

In this chapter, we'll see the following classical patterns:

- Components
- Singletons
- Observers

Components

In the first three chapters of this book, we saw a whole lot of Angular components. The Angular `Component` is one of the main building blocks of an Angular application with, for example, `services`, `pipes`, and so on. As a reminder, a TypeScript class becomes an Angular component using the following annotation:

```
import { Component } from '@angular/core';

@Component({
  selector: 'app-root',
  templateUrl: './app.component.html',
  styleUrls: ['./app.component.css']
})
export class AppComponent {
  title = 'app';
}
```

Here, the `AppComponent` class is supercharged with the behavior of the `selector`, `templateUrl`, and `styleUrls` Angular components.

Singleton

Another handy pattern to use for frontend applications is the singleton. The singleton ensures that only one instance of a given object exists in your program. Moreover, it provides a global point of access to the object.

Here's what it looks like in practice:

```
export class MySingleton{
    //The constructor is private so we
    //can't do `let singleton:MySingleton = new MySingleton();`
    private static instance:MySingleton = null;

    private constructor(){

    }

    public static getInstance():MySingleton{
        if(MySingleton.instance == null){
            MySingleton.instance = new MySingleton();
        }
```

```
        return MySingleton.instance;
    }
}
 let singleton:MySingleton = MySingleton.getInstance();
```

We have a class that has a `private static instance:MySingleton` attribute. Then, we have a private constructor that makes the following fail:

```
let singleton:MySingleton = new MySingleton();
```

Note that it fails because your TypeScript transpiler complains about the visibility. However, if you transpile the `MySingleton` class to JavaScript and import it into another TypeScript project, you'll be able to use the *new* operator because the transpiled TypeScript doesn't have any visibility.

The problem with this fairly simple implementation of the singleton pattern is concurrency. Indeed, if two processes hit `getInstance():MySingleton` at the same time, then we'll have two instances of `MySingleton` on the program. To be sure that doesn't happen, we can use a technique known as early instantiation:

```
export

 class MySingleton
 {
   private static instance : MySingleton = new MySingleton();

 private constructor()
  {
  }

 }

 singleton: MySingleton = MySingleton.getInstance();
```

While you can implement your singleton in TypeScript, you can also leverage the Angular way of creating a singleton: services! Indeed, in Angular, services are only instantiated once and injected to any components needing it. Here's an example of a service and injection via the `NgModule` we have seen before in this book:

```
 import { Injectable } from '@angular/core';

@Injectable()
export class ApiService {

  private static increment:number = 0;
  public constructor(){
    ApiService.increment++;
```

```
  }
  public toString() :string {
    return "Current instance: " + ApiService.increment;
  }

}

 // ./app.component.ts

 import { Component } from '@angular/core';
import { ApiService } from './api.service';

@Component({
  selector: 'app-root',
  templateUrl: './app.component.html',
  styleUrls: ['./app.component.css']
})
export class AppComponent {
  title = 'app';

  public constructor(api:ApiService){
    console.log(api);
  }
}


 // ./other/other.component.ts

 import { Component, OnInit } from '@angular/core';
import { ApiService } from './../api.service';

@Component({
  selector: 'app-other',
  templateUrl: './other.component.html',
  styleUrls: ['./other.component.css']
})
export class OtherComponent implements OnInit {

  public constructor(api:ApiService){
    console.log(api);
  }

  ngOnInit() {
  }

}
```

```
//app.module.ts

import { BrowserModule } from '@angular/platform-browser';
import { NgModule } from '@angular/core';
import { MySingleton } from './singleton';

import { AppComponent } from './app.component';
import { OtherComponent } from './other/other.component';

import { ApiService } from './api.service';

@NgModule({
  declarations: [
    AppComponent,
    OtherComponent
  ],
  imports: [
    BrowserModule
  ],
  providers: [ApiService],
  bootstrap: [AppComponent]
})
export class AppModule {

}
```

In the preceding code, we have the following:

- `APIService`, which displays the `@Injectable()` annotation that makes it, well, injectable. Also, the `APIService` has an `increment:number` attribute that is incremented every time a new instance is created. With `increment:number` being static, it'll tell us exactly how many instances there are in our program. Finally, `APIService` has a `toString:string` method that returns the current instance number.
- `AppComponent` is a classical component that receives an injection of `APIService`.
- `OtherComponent` is another classical component that receives an injection of `APIService`.

- /app.module.ts contains NgModule. In NgModule, most of the declarations shown here have already been discussed in this book. The novelty comes from the providers: [APIService] part. Here, we declare a provider for APIService itself. As APIService doesn't do anything too crazy, it suffices itself and can be provided by using a reference to the class. More complex services that, for example, themselves require injection, need custom-tailored providers.

Now, if we navigate to these two components, the result would be the following:

```
Current instance: 1
Current instance: 1
```

This proves that only an instance has been created and the same instance has been injected into both components. Hence, we have a singleton. However, this singleton, while convenient, isn't really safe. Why you ask? Well, APIService can also be provided at the component level, like so:

```
import { Component } from '@angular/core';
import { ApiService } from './api.service';

@Component({
  selector: 'app-root',
  templateUrl: './app.component.html',
  styleUrls: ['./app.component.css']
})
export class AppComponent {
  title = 'app';

  public constructor(api:ApiService){
    console.log(api);
  }
}
 // ./other.component.ts

 @Component({
  selector: 'app-root',
  templateUrl: './app.component.html',
  styleUrls: ['./app.component.css']
  providers: [APIService],
 })
 export class OtherComponent implements OnInit {

  public constructor(api:ApiService){
    console.log(api);
  }
```

```
  ngOnInit() {
  }

}
```

In such a case, two separate instances would be created, resulting in the following output:

```
Current instance: 1
Current instance: 2
```

Consequently, using Angular services, you can't enforce the singleton pattern, contrary to its plain TypeScript counterpart. Also, the plain TypeScript would be an order of magnitude faster than the Angular services, as we skip the injection process altogether. The exact number depends heavily on the CPU/RAM of your machine.

The only questions left to answer in the case of the singleton is when to use it or which implementation performs the best. The singleton enforces only one instance of a given class in your program. Consequently, it's a very good fit for any communication with a backend or any hardware access. For example, in the case of communication with a backend, it might be desirable to have only one `APIService` handling API keys, API limits, and `csrf` tokens across the board without having to make sure we pass the same instance of the service throughout all our components, model, and so on. In the case of hardware access, you might want to be sure that you have only one connection open to the webcam or the microphone of our users so that you can properly release them when you are done with them.

On the performance side, here are the results, in milliseconds, for each implementation. I ran each version 100 times, excluded the outliers (best and worst 5%), and averaged the remaining 90 calls in the following table:

Singleton Lazy	Singleton Early	Service Injection
196ms	183ms	186ms

The code I ran was the following:

```
import { Component } from '@angular/core';

import {MySingleton} from './singleton';
import { SingletonService } from './singleton.service';

@Component({
  selector: 'app-root',
  templateUrl: './app.component.html',
  styleUrls: ['./app.component.css']
})
export class AppComponent {
```

```
    title = 'app works!';

    constructor(private singleton:SingletonService){
      singleton.doStuff();
    }
    //OR
    constructor(){
      MySingleton.getInstance().doStuff();
    }
  }
```

For the experiment with the service injection, I had to add the following line in `app.module.ts: providers: [SingletonService].`

To my surprise, the results are fairly close from one approach to the other. The singleton implementation leveraging the early instantiation performs only 2% better than the more practical service injection. The singleton with the lazy instantiation is closing the podium with 196 ms (7% worse than singleton early instantiation and 5% worse than service injection).

Factory method

Let's assume that we have a `User` class with two private variables: `lastName:string` and `firstName:string`. In addition, this simple class proposes the `hello` method that prints `"Hi I am", this.firstName, this.lastName`:

```
    class User{
        constructor(private lastName:string, private firstName:string){
        }
        hello(){
            console.log("Hi I am", this.firstName, this.lastName);
        }
    }
```

Now, consider that we receive users through a JSON API. It'll more than likely look something like this:

```
    [{"lastName":"Nayrolles","firstName":"Mathieu"}...].
```

With the following snippet, we can create a `User`:

```
    let userFromJSONAPI: User =
    JSON.parse('[{"lastName":"Nayrolles","firstName":"Mathieu"}]')[0];
```

Until now, the TypeScript compiler doesn't complain, and it executes smoothly. It works because the `parse` method returns `any` (for example, the TypeScript equivalent of the Java object). Sure enough, we can convert the `any` into `User`. However, `userFromJSONAPI.hello();` will yield the following:

```
json.ts:19
 userFromJSONAPI.hello();
                 ^
 TypeError: userFromUJSONAPI.hello is not a function
     at Object.<anonymous> (json.ts:19:18)
     at Module._compile (module.js:541:32)
     at Object.loader (/usr/lib/node_modules/ts-node/src/ts-node.ts:225:14)
     at Module.load (module.js:458:32)
     at tryModuleLoad (module.js:417:12)
     at Function.Module._load (module.js:409:3)
     at Function.Module.runMain (module.js:575:10)
     at Object.<anonymous> (/usr/lib/node_modules/ts-node/src/bin/ts-
node.ts:110:12)
     at Module._compile (module.js:541:32)
     at Object.Module._extensions..js (module.js:550:10)
```

Why? Well, the left-hand side of assignation is defined as `User`, sure, but it'll be erased when we transpile it to JavaScript.

The type-safe TypeScript way to do it would be as follows:

```
let validUser =
JSON.parse('[{"lastName":"Nayrolles","firstName":"Mathieu"}]')
  .map((json: any):User => {
      return new User(json.lastName, json.firstName);
  })[0];
```

Interestingly enough, the type of function won't help you either. In both cases, it'll display `object` instead of `User`, as the very concept of user doesn't exist in JavaScript.

While the direct type-safe approach works, it isn't very expansible nor reusable. Indeed, the map callback method would have to be duplicated everywhere you receive a JSON user. The most convenient way to do that is through the `Factory` pattern. A Factory is used for objects without exposing the instantiation logic to the client.

If we were to have a factory to create a user, it would look like this:

```
export class POTOFactory{

    /**
     * Builds an User from json response
     * @param  {any}  jsonUser
     * @return {User}
     */
    static buildUser(jsonUser: any): User {

        return new User(
            jsonUser.firstName,
            jsonUser.lastName
        );
    }

}
```

Here, we have a `static` method, named `buildUser`, that receives a JSON object and take all the required value inside the JSON object to invoke, with the right attributes, a hypothetical `User` constructor. The method is static, like all the methods of such a factory are. Indeed, we don't need to save any states or instance-bound variables in a factory; we only encapsulate away the gruesome creation of users. Note that your factory will likely be shared with the rest of your POTOs.

Observer

The observable pattern that allows an object, called the subject, to keep track of other objects, called observers, is interested in the subject state. When the subject state changes, it notifies its observers. The mechanism behind this is really simple.

Let's take a look at the following observer/subject implementation in pure TypeScript (no Angular 2 or framework of any kind, just Typescript). First, I defined an `Observer` interface that any concrete implementation will have to implement:

```
export interface Observer{
    notify();
}
```

This interface only defines the `notify()` method. This method will be called by the subject (the object being observed by the observer) when its state changes. Then, I have an implementation of this interface, named `HumanObserver`:

```
export class HumanObserver implements Observer{
    constructor(private name:string){}

    notify(){

        console.log(this.name, 'Notified');
    }
}
```

This implementation leverages the TypeScript property constructor, where you can define the property of your class inside the constructor. This notation is 100% equivalent to the following while being shorter:

```
private name:string;
constructor(name:string){

        this.name = name;
}
```

Following the definitions of the `Observer` interface and the `HumanObserver`, we can move on to the subject. I defined a subject class that manages the observers. This class has three methods: `attachObserver`, `detachObserver`, and `notifyObservers`:

```
export class Subject{
private observers:Observer[] = [];

/**
 * Adding an observer to the list of observers
 */
attachObserver(observer:Observer):void{

        this.observers.push(observer);
}

/**
 * Detaching an observer
 */
detachObserver(observer:Observer):void{

    let index:number = this.observers.indexOf(observer);

    if(index > -1){
```

```
        this.observers.splice(index, 1);
    }else{

        throw "Unknown observer";

    }

}

/**
 * Notify all the observers in this.observers
 */
protected notifyObservers(){

    for (var i = 0; i < this.observers.length; ++i) {

        this.observers[i].notify();

    }

}

}
```

The attachObserver method pushes new observers into the observers property, while the detachObserver removes them.

Subject implementations are often found with attach/detach, subscribe/unsubscribe, or add/delete prefixes.

The last method is notifyObservers, which iterates over the observers and invokes their notify method. The last class allowing us to showcase the observable mechanism is IMDB, which extends subject. It will notify observers when a movie gets added:

```
export class IMDB extends Subject{

    private movies:string[] = [];

     public addMovie(movie:string){

         this.movies.push(movie);
         this.notifyObservers();

     }

  }
```

To make the pieces communicate with each other, we have to: create a Subject, create an Observer, attach the Observer to the Subject, and change the state of the subject via the addMovie method.

More concretely, here's an implementation of the previous list:

```
let imdb:IMDB = new IMDB();
 let mathieu:HumanObserver = new HumanObserver("Mathieu");
 imbd.attachObserver(mathieu);
 imbd.addMovie("Jaws");
```

To speed up our development process, we will install `ts-node`. This node package will transpile TypeScript files into JavaScript and resolve the dependencies between said files.

The output is `Mathieu Notified`. We can try to detach `mathieu` and add another movie:

```
imdb.detachObserver(mathieu);
 imdb.addMovie("Die Hard");
```

The output is still `Mathieu Notified`, which happens after we add the `Jaws` movie. The second movie addition (`Die Hard`) doesn't trigger a `Mathieu Notified` print to the console as it has been detached.

TypeScript observables with parameters

So, this is a basic implementation of the observer pattern. Nevertheless, it is not fully fledged as the `HumanObserver` only knows that something has changed in one of the subjects it observes. Consequently, it has to iterate over all of the subjects it observes and check their previous state against their current state to identify what has changed and where. A better way to go about this would be to modify the `notify` of the `Observer` so that it contains more information. For example, we could add optional parameters as follows:

```
export interface Observer{

    notify(value?:any, subject?:Subject);
 }

 export class HumanObserver implements Observer{

    constructor(private name:string){}

    notify(value?:any, subject?:Subject){

        console.log(this.name, 'received', value, 'from', subject);
    }
 }
```

The notify() method now accepts an optional value parameter, which characterizes the new state of the subject object. We can also receive a reference to the Subject object itself. This is useful in case the observer observes many subjects. In such a case, we need to be able to differentiate them. Accordingly, we have to change the Subject and IMDB a bit so that they use the new notify:

```
export class Subject{

    private observers:Observer[] = [];

    attachObserver(oberver:Observer):void{

        this.obervers.push(oberver);
    }

    detachObserver(observer:Observer):void{
        let index:number = this.obervers.indexOf(observer);
        if(index > -1){
            this.observers.splice(index, 1);

        }else{

            throw "Unknown observer";
        }
    }

    protected notifyObservers(value?:any){

        for (var i = 0; i < this.obervers.length; ++i) {

            this.observers[i].notify(value, this);
        }
    }
}

export class IMDB extends Subject{

    private movies:string[] = [];

    public addMovie(movie:string){

        this.movies.push(movie);
        this.notifyObservers(movie);
    }
}
```

Finally, the output is as follows:

```
Mathieu received Jaws from IMDB {

  observers: [ HumanObserver { name: 'Mathieu' } ],
  movies: [ 'Jaws' ] }
```

This is way more expressive than `Mathieu Notified`. Now, when we use `Observer` patterns for asynchronous programming, what we really mean is that we ask for something, and we do not want to wait to do anything during its processing. Instead, what we do is subscribe to the response event to be notified when the response comes. In the following sections, we will use the same pattern and mechanisms with Angular.

Observing HTTP responses

In this section, we will build a JSON API that returns movies according to search parameters. Instead of simply waiting for the HTTP query to complete, we will leverage the power of the observer design pattern to let the user know we are waiting and, if need be, execute other processes. First things first: we need a data source for our IMDB-like application. Building and deploying a server-side application that's able to interpret an HTTP query and send results accordingly is relatively simple nowadays. However, this falls outside the scope of this book. Instead, what we will do is fetch a static JSON file hosted at `http://bit.ly/mastering-angular2-marvel`. This file contains some of the latest movies of the Marvel Cinematic Universe. It contains a JSON array describing 14 movies as JSON objects. Here's the first movie:

```
{
"movie_id" : 1,
"title" : "The Incredible Hulk",
"phase" : "Phase One: Avengers Assembled",
"category_name" : "Action",
"release_year" : 2005,
"running_time" : 135,
"rating_name" : "PG-13",
"disc_format_name" : "Blu-ray",
"number_discs" : 1,
"viewing_format_name" : "Widescreen",
"aspect_ratio_name" : " 2.35:1",
"status" : 1,
"release_date" : "June 8, 2008",
"budget" : "150,000,000",
"gross" : "263,400,000",
"time_stamp" : "2018-06-08"
},
```

You can find standard information that an IMDB-like application would provide, such as release year, running time, and so on. Our goal is to design an asynchronous JSON API making each field searchable.

As we are fetching a static JSON file (we will not insert, update, or delete any elements), acceptable API calls would be as follows:

```
IMDBAPI.fetchOneById(1);
  IMDBAPI.fetchByFields(MovieFields.release_date, 2015);
```

The first call simply fetches the movie with `movie_id = 1`; the second call is a more generic one that works in any field. To prevent the API consumer from requesting fields that don't exist in our movie, we restrict the field values using an enumerator defined inside a `Movie` class. Now, the important part here is the actual return of these calls. Indeed, they will trigger an observable mechanism wherein the caller will attach him/herself to an observable HTTP call. Then, when the HTTP call is complete and the results have filtered according to the query parameter, the callee will notify the caller about the response. Consequently, the caller does not have to wait for the callee (`IMDBAPI`), as they will be notified when the request is complete.

Implementation

Let's dive into the implementation. First, we will need to create a new Angular project using the Angular CLI:

```
mkdir angular-observable
  ng init
  ng serve
```

Next, we will need a model to represent the movie concept. We will generate this class using the `ng g class` models/Movie command line. Then, we can add a constructor defining all the private fields of the `Movie` models, which is the same as we did for the getters and setters:

```
export class Movie {

    public constructor(
        private _movie_id:number,
        private _title: string,
        private _phase: string,
        private _category_name: string,
        private _release_year: number,
        private _running_time: number,
        private _rating_name: string,
```

```
            private _disc_format_name: string,
            private _number_discs: number,
            private _viewing_format_name: string,
            private _aspect_ratio_name: string,
            private _status: string,
            private _release_date: string,
            private _budget: number,
            private _gross: number,
            private _time_stamp:Date){
        }

     public toString = () : string => {

            return `Movie (movie_id: ${this._movie_id},
            title: ${this._title},
            phase: ${this._phase},
            category_name: ${this._category_name},
            release_year: ${this._release_year},
            running_time: ${this._running_time},
            rating_name: ${this._rating_name},
            disc_format_name: ${this._disc_format_name},
          number_discs: ${this._number_discs},
            viewing_format_name: ${this._viewing_format_name},
            aspect_ratio_name: ${this._aspect_ratio_name},
            status: ${this._status},
            release_date: ${this._release_date},
            budget: ${this._budget},
            gross: ${this._gross},
            time_stamp: ${this._time_stamp})`;

        }
    //GETTER
    //SETTER
}

export enum MovieFields{
    movie_id,
    title,
    phase,
    category_name,
    release_year,
    running_time,
    rating_name,
    disc_format_name,
    number_discs,
    viewing_format_name,
    aspect_ratio_name,
    status,
```

```
            release_date,
            budget,
            gross,
            time_stamp
    }
```

Here, each field of the movie JSON definition is mapped into a private member of the `Movie` class using the constructor property declaration

of TypeScript. We also override the `toString` method so that it prints every field. In the `toString` method, we take advantage of multi-line strings provided by the backtick (`` ` ``) and the `${}` syntax that allows the concatenation of strings and different variables. Then, we have an enumerator called `MovieFields` that will allow us to restrict the searchable field.

Moving on, we need to generate the `IMDBAPI` class. As the `IMDBAPI` class will be potentially used everywhere in our program, we will make it a service. The advantage is that services can be injected into any component or directive. Moreover, we can choose if we want Angular 2 to create an instance of the `IMDBAPI` per injection or always inject the same instance. If the provider for the `IMDBAPI` is created at the application level, then the same instance of the `IMDBAPI` will be served to anyone requesting it. At the component level, however, a new instance of the `IMDBAPI` will be created and served to the component each time the said component is instantiated. In our case, it makes more sense to have only one instance of the `IMDBAPI`, as it will not have any particular states that are susceptible to change from component to component. Let's generate the `IMDBAPI` service (`ng g s services/IMDBAPI`) and implement the two methods we defined earlier:

```
IMDBAPI.fetchOneById(1);
    IMDBAPI.fetchByFields(MovieFields.release_date, 2015);
```

Here's the IMDAPI service with the `fetchOneById` method:

```
import { Injectable } from '@angular/core';
 import { Http }  from '@angular/http';
 import { Movie, MovieFields } from '../models/movie';
 import { Observable } from 'rxjs/Rx';
 import 'rxjs/Rx';

 @Injectable()

 export class IMDBAPIService {

    private moviesUrl:string = "app/marvel-cinematic-universe.json";

    constructor(private http: Http) { }
```

```
/**
 * Return an Observable to a Movie matching id
 * @param   {number}         id
 * @return {Observable<Movie>}
 */
public fetchOneById(id:number):Observable<Movie>{
  console.log('fetchOneById', id);

      return this.http.get(this.moviesUrl)
      /**
       * Transforms the result of the HTTP get, which is observable
       * into one observable by item.
       */
      .flatMap(res => res.json().movies)

      /**
       * Filters movies by their movie_id

       */
      .filter((movie:any)=>{

          console.log("filter", movie);
          return (movie.movie_id === id)
      })

      /**
      * Map the JSON movie item to the Movie Model
      */
      .map((movie:any) => {

          console.log("map", movie);

          return new Movie(

              movie.movie_id,
              movie.title,
              movie.phase,
              movie.category_name,
              movie.release_year,
              movie.running_time,
              movie.rating_name,
              movie.disc_format_name,
              movie.number_discs,
              movie.viewing_format_name,
              movie.aspect_ratio_name,
              movie.status,
              movie.release_date,
              movie.budget,
```

```
                    movie.gross,
                    movie.time_stamp
               );
          });
    }
  }
```

Understanding the implementation

Let's break it down chunk by chunk. First, the declaration of the service is pretty standard:

```
import { Injectable } from '@angular/core';
import { Http } from '@angular/http';

import { Movie, MovieFields } from '../models/movie';
import { Observable } from 'rxjs/Rx';
import 'rxjs/Rx';

@Injectable()
  export class IMDBAPIService {
    private moviesUrl:string = "app/marvel-cinematic-universe.json";
    constructor(private http: Http) { }
```

Services are injectable. Consequently, we need to import and add the `@Injectable` annotation. We also import `Http`, `Movie`, `MovieFields`, `Observable`, and the operators of `Rxjs`. **RxJS** stands for **reactive extensions for JavaScript**. It is an API to perform observer, iterator, and functional programming. When it comes to asynchronism in Angular 2, you rely on RxJS for the most part.

One important thing to note is that we use RxJS 5.0, which is a complete rewrite, based on the same concept of RxJS 4.0.

`IMDBAPIService` also has a reference to the path of our JSON file and a constructor to receive an injection of the HTTP service. On the implementation of the `fetchOneById` method, we can see four distinct operations chained to each other: `get`, `flatMap`, `filter`, and `map`. Get returns an observable on the body of the HTTP request. `flatMap` transforms the `get Observable` by applying a function that you specify for each item emitted by the source `Observable`, where that function returns an `Observable` that emits items. `FlatMap` then merges the emissions of these resultant `Observables`, emitting these merged results as its sequence. In our case, it means that we will apply the next two operations (filter and map) on all the items received from the HTTP get. The filter checks if the ID of the current movie is the one we are looking to Map transform the JSON representation of a movie into the typeScript representation of a movie (such as the `Movie` class).

This last operation, while counter-intuitive, is mandatory. Indeed, one could think that the JSON representation and the TypeScript representation are identical as they own the same fields. However, the TypeScript representation, as well as its properties, define functions such as `toString`, the getters, and the setters. Removing the map would return an `Object` instance containing all the fields of `Movie` without being one. Also, a typecast will not help you there. Indeed, the TypeScript transpiler will allow you to cast an `Object` into a `Movie`, but it still won't have the methods defined in the `Movie` class as the concept of static typing disappears when the TypeScript is transpiled into JavaScript. The following would fail to transpile at execution time:

```
movie.movie_id(25) TypeError: movie.movie_id is not a function at
Object.<anonymous>
movie: Movie = JSON.parse(`{
                        "movie_id" : 1,
                        "title" : "Iron Man",
                        "phase" : "Phase One: Avengers Assembled",
                        "category_name" : "Action",
                        "release_year" : 2015,
                        "running_time" : 126,
                        "rating_name" : "PG-13",
                        "disc_format_name" : "Blu-ray",
                        "number_discs" : 1,
                        "viewing_format_name" : "Widescreen",
                        "aspect_ratio_name" : " 2.35:1",
                        "status" : 1,
                        "release_date" : "May 2, 2008",
                        "budget" : "140,000,000",
                        "gross" : "318,298,180",
                        "time_stamp" : "2015-05-03"
            }`);
Console.log(movie.movie_id(25));
```

Now, if we want to use our IMDB service, further modifications of the code that was generated by the Angular CLI is required. First, we need to modify `main.ts` so that it looks like this:

```
import{ bootstrap } from '@angular/platform-browser-dynamic';
import{ enableProdMode } from '@angular/core';
import{ AngularObservableAppComponent, environment } from './app/';
import{ IMDBAPIService } from './app/services/imdbapi.service';
import { HTTP_PROVIDERS } from '@angular/http';
if(environment.production) {
    enableProdMode();
}
```

```
bootstrap(AngularObservableAppComponent,
    [IMDBAPIService , HTTP_PROVIDERS]
);
```

The lines in bold represent what has been added. We import our `IMDBService` and the `HTTP_PROVIDERS`. Both providers are declared at the application level, meaning that the instance that will be injected into the controller or directive will always be the same.

Then, we modify the `angular-observable.component.ts` file that was generated and add the following:

```
import { Component } from '@angular/core';
import { IMDBAPIService } from './services/imdbapi.service';
import { Movie } from './models/movie';

@Component({
  moduleId: module.id,
  selector: 'angular-observable-app',
  templateUrl: 'angular-observable.component.html',
  styleUrls: ['angular-observable.component.css']
})
export class AngularObservableAppComponent {
  title = 'angular-observable works!';
  private movies:Movie[] = [];
  private error:boolean = false;
  private finished:boolean = false;

constructor(private IMDBAPI:IMDBAPIService){
  this.IMDBAPI.fetchOneById(1).subscribe(
    value => {this.movies.push(value); console.log("Component",value)},
    error => this.error = true,
    () => this.finished =true
  )
 }
}
```

We have added several properties to `AngularObservableAppComponent`: `movies`, `error`, and `finished`. The first property is an array of `Movie` that will store the result of our queries, and the second and the third properties flag for `error` and `termination`. In the constructor, we have an injection of `IMDBAPIService`, and we subscribe to the result of the `fetchOneById` method. The `subscribe` method expects three callbacks:

- **Observer:** Receives the value yield by the observed method. It is the RxJS equivalent of the notifying method we saw earlier in this chapter.
- **Error (Optional)**: Triggered in the case that the observed object yields an error.
- **Complete (Optional)**: Triggered on completion.

Finally, we can modify the `angular-observable.component.html` file to map the `movie` property of the `AngularObservableAppComponent` array:

```html
<h1>
  {{title}}
</h1>

<ul>
    <li *ngFor = "let movie of movies">{{movie}}</li>
</ul>
```

We can see that the first movie item has been correctly inserted into our `ul/li` HTML structure. What's really interesting about this code is the order in which things execute. Analyzing the log helps us to grasp the true power of asynchronism in Angular with RxJS. Here's what the console looks like after the execution of our code:

```
javascript fetchOneById 1 :4200/app/services/imdbapi.service.js:30 filter
Object :4200/app/services/imdbapi.service.js:34 map Object
:4200/app/angular-observable.component.js:21 Component
Movie_aspect_ratio_name: " 2.35:1"_budget: "140,000,000"_category_name:
"Action"_disc_format_name: "Blu-ray"_gross: "318,298,180"_movie_id:
1_number_discs: 1_phase: "Phase One: Avengers Assembled"_rating_name:
"PG-13"_release_date: "May 2, 2008"_release_year: 2015_running_time:
126_status: 1_time_stamp: "2015-05-03"_title: "Iron
Man"_viewing_format_name: "Widescreen"aspect_ratio_name: (...)budget:
(...)category_name: (...)disc_format_name: (...)gross: (...)movie_id:
(...)number_discs: (...)phase: (...)rating_name: (...)release_date:
(...)release_year: (...)running_time: (...)status: (...)time_stamp:
(...)title: (...)toString: ()viewing_format_name: (...)__proto__: Object
:4200/app/services/imdbapi.service.js:30 filter Object
:4200/app/services/imdbapi.service.js:30 filter Object
:4200/app/services/imdbapi.service.js:30 filter Object
:4200/app/services/imdbapi.service.js:30 filter Object
:4200/app/services/imdbapi.service.js:30 filter Object
:4200/app/services/imdbapi.service.js:30 filter Object
:4200/app/services/imdbapi.service.js:30 filter Object
:4200/app/services/imdbapi.service.js:30 filter Object
:4200/app/services/imdbapi.service.js:30 filter Object
:4200/app/services/imdbapi.service.js:30 filter Object
:4200/app/services/imdbapi.service.js:30 filter Object
:4200/app/services/imdbapi.service.js:30 filter Object
:4200/app/services/imdbapi.service.js:30 filter Object
:4200/app/services/imdbapi.service.js:30 filter Object
```

As you can see, `AngularObservableAppComponent` was notified that a movie matching the query was found before the filter function analyzed all the items. As a reminder, the order of operations inside `fetchOneById` by ID was: `get`, `flatMap`, `filter`, and `map`, and we have a logging statement in the `filter` and `map` method as well. So, here, the `filter` operation analyzes the first item, which happens to be the one we look for (`movie_id===1`), and forwards it to the map operations that transform it into a `Movie`. This `Movie` is sent right away to `AngularObservableAppComponent`. We can clearly see that the received object in the `AngularObservableAppComponent` component is from the `Movie` type as the console gives us our overriding of the `toString` method. Then, the filter operation continues with the rest of the items. None of them match. Consequently, we do not have any more notifications. Let's test this further with a second method, `IMDBAPI.fetchByField`:

```
public fetchByField(field:MovieFields, value:any){
console.log('fetchByField', field, value);
return this.http.get (this.moviesUrl)
    .flatMap(res => res.json().movies)
/**
* Filters movies by their field
*/
.filter((movie:any) =>{

    console.log("filter" , movie);
    return (movie[MovieFields[field]] === value)
 })

/**
* Map the JSON movie item to the Movie Model
*/
.map(( movie: any) => {
    console.log ("map", movie);
    return new Movie(
        movie.movie_id,
        movie.title,
        movie.phase,
        movie.category_name,
        movie.release_year,
        movie.running_time,
        movie.rating_name,
        movie.disc_format_name,
        movie.number_discs,
        movie.viewing_format_name,
        movie.aspect_ratio_name,
        movie.status,
        movie.release_date,
        movie.budget,
```

```
            movie.gross,
            movie.time_stamp
        );
    });
}
```

For the `fetchByField` method, we use the same mechanisms as the `fetchById`. Unsurprisingly, the operations stay the same: `get`, `flatMap`, `filter`, and `map`. The only change is in the filter operation, where we now have to filter on a field that's received as a parameter:

```
return (movie[MovieFields[field]] === value).
```

This statement can be a bit overwhelming to the TypeScript or JavaScript newcomer. First, the `MovieFields[field]` part is explained by the fact that `enum` will be transpiled into the following JavaScript function:

```
(function(MovieFields) {
    MovieFields[MovieFields["movie_id"] = 0] = "movie_id";
    MovieFields[MovieFields["title"] = 1] = "title";
    MovieFields[MovieFields["phase"] = 2] = "phase";
    MovieFields[MovieFields["category_name"] = 3] = "category_name";
    MovieFields[MovieFields["release_year"] = 4] = "release_year";
    MovieFields[MovieFields["running_time"] = 5] = "running_time";
    MovieFields[MovieFields["rating_name"] = 6] = "rating_name";
    MovieFields[MovieFields["disc_format_name"] = 7] ="disc_format_name";
    MovieFields[MovieFields["number_discs"] = 8] = "number_discs";
    MovieFields[MovieFields["viewing_format_name"] = 9] =
"viewing_format_name";
 MovieFields[MovieFields["aspect_ratio_name"] = 10] =  "aspect_ratio_name";
 MovieFields[MovieFields["status"] = 11] = "status";
 MovieFields[MovieFields["release_date"] = 12] = "release_date";
 MovieFields[MovieFields["budget"] = 13] = "budget";
 MovieFields[MovieFields["gross"] = 14] = "gross";
 MovieFields[MovieFields["time_stamp"] = 15] = "time_stamp";
 })(exports.MovieFields || (exports.MovieFields =  {}));
 var MovieFields = exports.MovieFields;
```

Consequently, the value of `MovieFields.release_year` is, in fact, 4, and `MovieFields` is a static array. Consequently, requesting the fourth index of the `MovieFields` array gives me the string `release_year is`. So, `movie[MovieFields[field]]` is interpreted as a `movie["release_year is"]` in our current example.

Now, we have five matches instead of one. Upon analysis of the console, we can see that the notifications still come as soon as a suitable object is found and not when they have all been filtered:

```
fetchByField 4 2015
  imdbapi.service.js:43  filter Object  {movie_id: 1,  title: "Iron Man",
phase: "Phase One: Avengers Assembled", category_name: "Action",
release_year: 2015...}
  imdbapi.service.js:47 map Object {movie_id: 1, title: "Iron Man", phase:
"Phase One: Avengers Assembled", category_name: "Action",  release_year:
2015...}
  angular-observable.component.js:22 Component Movie {_movie_id: 1, _title:
"Iron Man", _phase: "Phase One: Avengers Assembled", _category_name:
"Action", _release_year: 2015...}
  imdbapi.service.js:43 filter Object {movie_id: 2, title: "The Incredible
Hulk", phase: "Phase One: Avengers Assembled", category_name: "Action",
release_year: 2008...}
  imdbapi.service.js:43 filter Object {movie_id: 3, title: "Iron Man 2",
phase: "Phase One: Avengers Assembled", category_name: "Action",
release_year: 2015...}
  imdbapi.service.js:47map Object {movie_id: 3 =, title: "Iron Man 2",
phase: "Phase One: Avengers Assembled", category_name: "Action",
release_year: 2015...}
  angular-observable.component.js:22 Component Movie{_movie_id: 3, _title:
"Iron Man 2", _phase: "Phase One: Avengers Assembled", _category_name:
"Action", _release_year:2015...}
  imdbapi.service.js:43 filter Object {movie_id: 4, title: "Thor", phase:
"Phase One: Avengers Assembled", category_name: "Action",
release_year:2011...}
  imdbapi.service.js:43filter Object {movie_id: 5, title: "Captain America",
phase: "Phase One: Avengers Assembled", category_name: "Action",
release_year: 2011...}
  imdbapi.service.js:43 filter Object {movie_id: 6, title: "Avengers, The",
phase: "Phase One: Avengers Assembled", category_name: "Science Fiction",
release_year: 2012...}
  imdbapi.service.js:43 filter Object {movie_id: 7, title: "Iron Man 3",
phase: "Phase Two", category_name: "Action", release_year : 2015...}
  imdbapi.service.js:47 map Object {movie_id: 7, title: "Iron Man 3", phase:
"Phase Two", category_name: "Action", release_year:2015...}
  angular-observable.component.js: 22 Component Movie {_movie_id: 7, _title:
"Iron Man 3", _phase: "Phase Two", _category_name:"Action", _release_year:
2015...}
  imdbapi.service.js:43 filter Object {movie_id: 8, title: "Thor: The Dark
World", phase: "Phase Two", category_name: "Science Fiction", release_year:
2013...}
  imdbapi.service.js:43 filter Object {movie_id: 9, title: "Captain America:
The Winter Soldier", phase: "Phase Two", category_name: "Action",
release_year: 2014...}
```

```
imdbapi.service.js:43 filter Object {movie_id: 10, title: "Guardians of
the Galaxy", phase: "Phase Two", category_name: "Science Fiction",
release_year: 2014...}
 imdbapi.service.js:43 filter Object {movie_id: 11, title: "Avengers: Age
of Ultron", phase: "Phase Two", category_name: "Science Fiction",
release_year: 2015...}
 imdbapi.service.js:47 map Object {movie_id: 11, title: "Avengers: Age of
Ultron", phase:  "Phase Two", category_name: "Science Fiction",
release_year: 2015...}
 angular-observable.component.js:22 Component Movie {_movie_id: 11, _title:
"Avengers: Age of Ultron", _phase: "Phase Two", _category_name: "Science
Fiction", _release_year:2015...}
 imdbapi.service.js:43 filter Object {movie_id: 12, title: "Ant-Man",
phase: "Phase Two", category_name: "Science Fiction", release_year:
2015...}
 imdbapi.service.js:47 map Object {movie_id: 12, title: "Ant-Man", phase:
"Phase Two", category_name: "Science Fiction", release_year: 2015...}
 angular-observable.component.js:22 Component Movie {_movie_id: 12, _title:
"Ant-Man", _phase: "Phase Two", _category_name: "Science Fiction",
_release_year: 2015...}
 imdbapi.service.js:43 filter Object {movie_id: 13, title: "Captain
America: Civil War",phase: "Phase Three", category_name: "Science Fiction",
release_year: 2016...}
imdbapi.service.js:43 filter Object {movie_id: 14, title: "Doctor Strange",
phase: "Phase Two", category_name: "Science Fiction", release_year:
2016...}
```

Now, the other strength of this design pattern is the ability to unsubscribe yourself. To do so, you only have to acquire a reference to your subscription and call the `unsubscribe()` method, as follows:

```
constructor(private IMDBAPI:IMDBAPIService{
  let imdbSubscription =
  this.IMDBAPI.fetchByField(MovieFields.release_year, 2015).subscribe(
        value=> {
                this.movies.push(value);
                console.log("Component", value)
                if(this.movies.length > 2){
                        imdbSubscription.unsubscribe();
                }
        },
     error => this.error = true,
     () => this.finished = true
    );
  }
```

Here, we unsubscribe after the third notification. To add to all this, the observable object will even detect that nobody's observing it anymore and will stop whatever it was doing. Indeed, the previous code with `unsubscribe` produces:

```
fetchByField 4 2015
  imdbapi.service.js:43 filter Object {movie_id: 1, title: "Iron Man",
phase: "Phase One: Avengers Assembled", category_name: "Action",
release_year: 2015...}
  imdbapi.service.js:49 map Object {movie_id: 1, title: "Iron Man", phase:
"Phase One: Avengers Assembled", category_name: "Action", release_year:
2015...}
  angular-observable.component.js:24 Component Movie {_movie_id: 1, _title:
"Iron Man", _phase: "Phase One: Avengers Assembled", _category_name:
"Action", _release_year: 2015...}
  imdbapi.service.js:43 filter Object {movie_id: 2, title: "The Incredible
Hulk", phase: "Phase One: Avengers Assembled", category_name: "Action",
release_year: 2008...}
  imdbapi.service.js:43 filter Object { movie_id: 3, title: "Iron Man 2",
phase: "Phase One: Avengers Assembled", category_name: "Action",
release_year: 2015...}
  imdbapi.service.js:49 map Object {movie_id: 3, title: "Iron Man 2", phase:
"Phase One: Avengers Assembled", category_name: "Action", release_year:
2015...}
  angular-observable.component.js:24 Component Movie {_movie_id: 3, _title:
"Iron Man 2", _phase:  "Phase One: Avengers Assembled", _category_name:
"Action",_release_year: 2015...}
  imdbapi.service.js:43 filter Object {movie_id: 4, title: "Thor", phase:
"Phase One: Avengers Assembled", category_name: "Action", release_year:
2011...}
  imdbapi.service.js:43 filter Object {movie_id: 5, title: "Captain
America", phase: "Phase One: Avengers Assembled", category_name:
"Action",release_year: 2011...}
  imdbapi.service.js:43 filter Object {movie_id: 6, title: "Avengers, The",
phase: "Phase One: Avengers Assembled", category_name: "Science Fiction",
release_year: 2012...}
  imdbapi.service.js:43 filter Object {movie_id: 7, title: "Iron Man 3",
phase: "Phase Two", category_name: "Action", release_year: 2015...}
  imdbapi.service.js:49 map Object {movie_id: 7, title: "Iron Man 3", phase:
"Phase Two", category_name: "Action", release_year: 2015...}
  angular-observable.component.js:24 Component Movie {_movie_id: 7, _title:
"Iron Man 3", _phase: "Phase Two", _category_name: "Action", _release_year:
2015...}
```

Everything stops after the third notification.

Promises

The promise is another useful asynchronous concept that has been provided by Angular 2. It promises to provide the same feature as `Observer`: process something and, asynchronously, notify the caller that an answer is available. So, why bother having two concepts that do the same thing? Well, the verbosity of `Observer` allows one thing that the `Promise` does not: unsubscribe. Consequently, if you never plan on using the unsubscribe capacity of the observer pattern, you are better off using `Promises`, which are, in my opinion, more intuitive in their writing and understanding. To emphasize the differences between observers and promises, we will take the same example as before—fetching movies from a JSON API. `AngularObservableAppComponent` will make an asynchronous call to `IMDBAPIService` and, upon the answer, will update the HTML view.

Here's the `fetchOneById` method using `Promise` instead of `Observable`:

```
/**
 * Return a Promise to a Movie matching id
 *@param  {number}  id
 *@return {Promise<Movie>}
 */
public fetchOneById(id:number) : Promise <Movie>{
console.log('fecthOneById', id);

    return this.http.get(this.moviesUrl)
  /**
   * Transforms the result of the HTTP get, which is observable
   * into one observable by item.
   */
  .flatMap(res => res.json().movies)
  /**
   * Filters movies by their movie_id
   */
  .filter((movie:any) =>{
     console.log("filter", movie);
     return (movie.movie_id === id)
})
  .toPromise()
  /**
* Map the JSON movie item to the Movie Model
*/
  .then((movie:any) => {

     console.log("map", movie);
     return new Movie(
          movie.movie_id,
          movie.title,
```

```
                        movie.phase,
                        movie.category_name,
                        movie.release_year,
                        movie.running_time,
                        movie.rating_name,
                        movie.disc_format_name,
                        movie.number_discs,
                        movie.viewing_format_name,
                        movie.aspect_ratio_name,
                        movie.status,
                        movie.release_date,
                        movie.budget,
                        movie.gross,
                        movie.time_stamp
              )
        });
        }
```

As shown by this code, we went from `flatMap`, `filter`, `map`, to `flatMap`, `filter`, to `Promise`, `then`. The new operations, `toPromise` and `then`, are creating a `Promise` object that will contain the result of the `filter` operation and, on completion of the `filter` operation, the `then` operation will be executed. The `then` operation can be thought of as a map; it does the same thing. To use this code, we also have to change the way we call `IMDBAPIService` in `AngularObservableAppComponent` to the following:

```
this.IMDBAPI.fetchOneById(1).then(
        value => {
                this.movies.push(value);

                console.log("Component", value)
        },
        error => this.error = true
);
```

Once again, we can see a `then` operation that will be executed when the promise from `IMDBAPIService.FetchOneById` has completed. The `then` operation accepts two callbacks: `onCompletion` and `onError`. The second callback, `onError`, is optional. Now, the `onCompletion` callback will only be executed once, when the Promise has completed, as shown in the console:

```
imdbapi.service.js:30 filter Object {movie_id: 2, title: "The Incredible
Hulk", phase: "Phase One: Avengers Assembled", category_name: "Action",
release_year: 2008...}
  imdbapi.service.js:30 filter Object {movie_id: 3, title: "Iron Man 2",
phase : "Phase One: Avengers Assembled", category_name: "Action",
release_year: 2015...}
```

```
  imdbapi.service.js:30 filter Object {movie_id: 4, title: "Thor", phase:
"Phase One: Avengers Assembled", category_name: "Action", release_year:
2011...}
  imdbapi.service.js:30 filter Object {movie_id: 5, title: "Captain
America", phase:  "Phase One: Avengers Assembled", category_name: "Action",
release_year: 2011...}
  imdbapi.service.js:30 filter Object {movie_id: 6, title: "Avengers, The",
phase: "Phase One: Avengers Assembled", category_name:"Science Fiction",
release_year: 2012...}
  imdbapi.service.js:30 filter Object {movie_id: 7, title: "Iron Man 3",
phase: "Phase Two", category_name: "Action", release_year: 2015...}
  imdbapi.service.js:30 filter Object {movie_id: 8, title: "Thor: The Dark
World", phase: "Phase Two", category_name: "Science Fiction", release_year:
2013...}
  imdbapi.service.js:30 filter Object {movie_id: 9, title: "Captain America:
The Winter Soldier", phase: "Phase Two", category_name:
"Action",release_year: 2014...}
  imdbapi.service.js:30 filter Object {movie_id: 10, title: "Guardians of
the Galaxy", phase: "Phase Two", category_name: "Science Fiction",
release_year: 2014...}
  imdbapi.service.js:30 filter Object { movie_id: 11, title: "Avengers: Age
of Ultron", phase: "Phase Two", category_name: "Science Fiction",
release_year: 2015...}
  imdbapi.service.js:30 filter Object {movie_id: 12, title: "Ant-Man",
phase: "Phase Two", category_name: "Science Fiction", release_year:
2015...}
  imdbapi.service.js:30 filter Object {movie_id: 13, title: "Captain
America: Civil War", phase: "Phase Three", category_name: "Science
Fiction", release_year: 2016...}
  imdbapi.service.js:30 filter Object {movie_id: 14, title: "Doctor
Strange", phase: "Phase Two", category_name: "Science Fiction",
release_year: 2016...}
  imdbapi.service.js:35 map Object {movie_id: 1, title: "Iron Man", phase:
"Phase One: Avengers Assembled", category_name: "Action", release_year:
2015...}
  angular-observable.component.js:23 Component Movie {_movie_id: 1, _title:
"Iron Man", _phase: "Phase One: Avengers Assembled", _category_name:
"Action",  _release_year: 2015...}
```

While the modification of IMDBAPIService was minimal for the fetchOneById method, we will have to change fetchByField more significantly. Indeed, the onComplete callback will only be executed once, so we need to return an array of Movie and not only one Movie. Here's the implementation of the fetchByField method:

```
public fetchByField(field: MovieFields, value: any) :Promise<Movie[]>{
        console.log('fetchByField', field, value);
        return this.http.get(this.moviesUrl)
```

```
         .map(res => res.json().movies.filter(
            (movie)=>{
                return (movie[MovieFields[field]] === value)
            })
        )
        .toPromise()
        /**
         * Map the JSON movie items to the Movie Model
         */
        .then((jsonMovies:any[]) => {
            console.log("map",jsonMovies);
            let movies:Movie[] = [];
            for (var i = 0; i < jsonMovies.length; i++) {
                movies.push(
                    new Movie(
                        jsonMovies[i].movie_id,
                        jsonMovies[i].title,
                        jsonMovies[i].phase,
                        jsonMovies[i].category_name,
                        jsonMovies[i].release_year,
                        jsonMovies[i].running_time,
                        jsonMovies[i].rating_name,
                        jsonMovies[i].disc_format_name,
                        jsonMovies[i].number_discs,
                        jsonMovies[i].viewing_format_name,
                        jsonMovies[i].aspect_ratio_name,
                        jsonMovies[i].status,
                        jsonMovies[i].release_date,
                        jsonMovies[i].budget,
                        jsonMovies[i].gross,
                        jsonMovies[i].time_stamp
                    )
                )
            }
            return movies;
        });
}
```

To implement this, I trade `flatMap` for a classical map as the first operation. In the map, I directly acquire the reference to the JSON `movie` array and apply the filed filter. The result is transformed into a promise and processed in `then`. The `then` operation receives an array of JSON `movies` and transforms it into an array of `Movie`. This produces an array of `Movie` which is returned, as the promised result, to the caller. The call in `AngularObservableAppComponent` is also a bit different, as we now expect an array:

```
this.IMDBAPI.fetchByField(MovieFields.release_year, 2015).then(
    value => {
```

```
        this.movies = value;
        console.log("Component", value)
    },
    error => this.error = true
)
```

Another way to use `Promise` is through the fork/join paradigm. Indeed, it is possible to launch many processes (fork) and wait for all the promises to complete before sending the aggregated result to the caller (join). It is therefore relatively easy to supercharge the `fetchByField` method, as it can run in many fields with logic or. Here are the three very short methods we need to implement to logic or:

```
/**
 * Private member storing pending promises
 */
private promises:Promise<Movie[]>[] = [];
/**
  * Register one promise for field/value. Returns this
  * for chaining i.e.
  *
  * byField(Y, X)
  * .or(...)
  * .fetch()
  *
  * @param {MovieFields} field
  * @param {any}         value
  * @return {IMDBAPIService}
  */
public byField(field:MovieFields, value:any):IMDBAPIService{

   this.promises.push(this.fetchByField(field, value));
   return this;
}
/**
 * Convenient method to make the calls more readable, i.e.
 *
 * byField(Y, X)
 * .or(...)
 * .fetch()
 *
 * instead of
 *
 * byField(Y, X)
 * .byField(...)
 * .fetch()
 *
 * @param {MovieFields} field
```

```
  * @param {any}          value
  * @return {IMDBAPIService}
  */
 public or(field:MovieFields, value:any):IMDBAPIService{
  return this.byField(field, value);

 }

 /**
  * Join all the promises and return the aggregated result.
  *
  *@return {Promise<Movie[]>}
  */
 public fetch():Promise<Movie[]>{
  return Promise.all(this.promises).then((results:any) => {
        //result is an array of movie arrays. One array per
        //promise. We need to flatten it.
        return [].concat.apply([], results);
  });
 }
```

Here, I provide two convenient methods, field and or, that take a MovieField and a value as an argument and create a new promise. They both return this for chaining. The fetch method joins all the promises together and merges their respective results. In AngularObservableAppComponent, we now have the following:

```
this.IMDBAPI.byField(MovieFields.release_year, 2015)
          .or(MovieFields.release_year, 2014)
          .or(MovieFields.phase, "Phase Two")
          .fetch()
          .then (
             value => {
                this.movies = value;
                console.log("Component", value)
             },
          error => this.error = true
      );
```

This is very simple to read and understand while keeping all the asynchronism capabilities of Angular 2.

Summary

In this chapter, we learned how to use some of the most useful classical patterns: component, singleton, and observer. We learned how to do it in pure TypeScript as well as by using Angular 2 building blocks. The code for this chapter can be found here: `https://github.com/MathieuNls/Angular-Design-Patterns-and-Best-Practices/tree/master/chap4`.

In the next chapter, we'll focus on patterns, aiming to ease and organize navigation in our Angular 2 application.

4
Navigational Patterns

In this chapter, we'll explore some of the most useful navigational object-oriented patterns and learn how to apply them in the Angular way. Navigational patterns are used to organize events that are related to the navigation of our users on our apps.

Angular is, by itself, an object-oriented framework, and it forces you to do most of your development in certain ways. For example, you are required to have components, services, pipes, and so on. Forcing these building blocks upon you contributes to building a good architecture, very much like what the Zend framework does for PHP, or Ruby on Rails for Ruby. Of course, in addition, frameworks are here to make your life easier and speed up development time.

While the Angular way of designing things is way above average, we can always do better. I do not claim that what I present in this chapter are the ultimate designs and that you will be able to use them to resolve anything from bakery one-pagers to dashboards for the Mars One mission—such a design doesn't exist, unfortunately—but it will definitively improve your toolbelt.

In this chapter, we will learn about the following patterns:

- Model-view-controller
- Redux

MVC

Oh MVC, good ol' MVC. You served us well for many years. Now, people want you to retire, without fuss if possible. Even I can see how younger, unidirectional user interface architectures can outsmart you and make you look like a relic from the past.

In this section, we'll first describe what the model-view-controller is, regardless of the programming language used to implement it, and then we'll see the shortcomings of applying MVC for frontend programming. Finally, I'll present a way of implementing an MVC that makes sense with Angular in terms of ease of implementation, maintenance, and performance.

Model-view-controller at large

The whole principle behind the model-view-controller design pattern is relatively simple. Indeed, as shown in the following diagram, it's composed of three blocks: **Model**, **View**, and **Controller**:

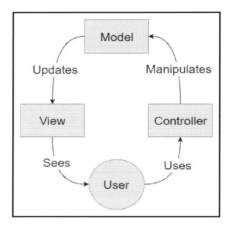

Model-view-controller overview

The components are as follows:

- The **Model** stores the data required by the application according to commands sent by the Controller.
- The **Controller** receives actions from the user (such as the click of a button) and directs model updates accordingly. It can also switch which view is used at any given moment.
- The **View** is generated and updated every time the model changes.

And that's it.

Let's see what a simple MVC implementation would look like in pure TypeScript.

First, let's define a `Movie` class like we did back in Chapter 3, *Classical Patterns*. In this version of the `Movie` class, we only have two attributes: `title` and `release_year`, which are defined using a TypeScript constructor:

```
class Movie{
    constructor(private title:string, private release_year:number){}
    public getTitle():string{
        return this.title;
    }
    public getReleaseYear():number{
        return this.release_year;
    }
}
```

Then, we define a `Model` class that imports the `movie.ts` file, containing the `Movie` class, using the `reference` keyword. This model class, which will be responsible for updating the view, has a movie array and two methods. The first method, `addMovie(title:string, year:number)`, is `public` and appends a new movie at the end of the `movies` attribute. It also calls the second method of the class, `appendView(movie:Movie)`, which is `private`. This second method manipulates the view as per model-view-controller definition. The view manipulation is rather simple: we append a new `li` tag to the `#movie` element of the view. The content of the newly created `li` tag is a concatenation of the movie title and release year:

```
/// <reference path="./movie.ts"/>

class Model{
    private movies:Movie[] = [];

    constructor(){
    }

    public addMovie(title:string, year:number){
        let movie:Movie = new Movie(title, year);
        this.movies.push(movie);
        this.appendView(movie);
    }

    private appendView(movie:Movie){
        var node = document.createElement("LI");
        var textnode = document.createTextNode(movie.getTitle() + "-" +
movie.getReleaseYear());
```

```
        node.appendChild(textnode);
        document.getElementById("movies").appendChild(node);
    }

}
```

We can now define a controller for our pure TypeScript model-view-controller. The controller has a `private model:Model` attribute that is initiated in the constructor. In addition, a `click` method is defined. This method takes a `string` and a `number` in parameters for the title and the release year, respectively. As you can see, the `click` method forwards the title and the release year to the `addMovie` method of the model. Then, the controller's job is done. It does not manipulate the view. You'll also notice the last line of the `controller.ts` file: `let controller = new Controller();`. This line allows us to create an instance of the controller that the view can bind to:

```
/// <reference path="./model.ts"/>

class Controller{
    private model:Model;

    constructor(){

        this.model = new Model();
    }

    click(title:string, year:number){

        console.log(title, year);
        this.model.addMovie(title, year);

    }

}
let controller = new Controller();
```

The last piece of our model-view-controller implementation would be the view. We have a bare-bones HTML form that, on submit, invokes the following:
`controller.click(this.title.value, this.year.value); return false;`.
`controller` has been defined in the `controller.ts` file with `let controller = new Controller();`. Then, for the parameters, we send `this.title.value` and `this.year.value`, where `this` refers to `<form>`. `title` and `year` refer to the fields for the title and the release year of the movie, respectively. We must also add `return false;` to prevent the page from reloading. Indeed, the default behavior of an HTML form, on submit, is to navigate to the action URL:

```
<html>
    <head>
        <script src="mvc.js"></script>
    </head>
    <body>
        <h1>Movies</h1>

        <div id="movies">

        </div>

        <form action="#" onsubmit="controller.click(this.title.value,
this.year.value); return false;">
            Title: <input name="title" type="text" id="title">
            Year: <input name="year" type="text" id="year">
          <input type="submit">
        </form>
    </body>
</html>
```

In the header, we add the `mvc.js` script generated by the following command: `tsc --out mvc.js controller.ts model.ts movie.ts`. The generated JavaScript looks like the following:

```
var Movie = /** @class */ (function () {
    function Movie(title, release_year) {
        this.title = title;
        this.release_year = release_year;
    }
    Movie.prototype.getTitle = function () {
        return this.title;
    };
    Movie.prototype.getReleaseYear = function () {
        return this.release_year;
    };
    return Movie;
}());
/// <reference path="./movie.ts"/>
var Model = /** @class */ (function () {
    function Model() {
        this.movies = [];
    }
    Model.prototype.addMovie = function (title, year) {
        var movie = new Movie(title, year);
        this.movies.push(movie);
        this.appendView(movie);
    };
    Model.prototype.appendView = function (movie) {
```

```
        var node = document.createElement("LI");
        var textnode = document.createTextNode(movie.getTitle() + "-" +
movie.getReleaseYear());
        node.appendChild(textnode);
        document.getElementById("movies").appendChild(node);
    };
    return Model;
}());
/// <reference path="./model.ts"/>
var Controller = /** @class */ (function () {
    function Controller() {
        this.model = new Model();
    }
    Controller.prototype.click = function (title, year) {
        console.log(title, year);
        this.model.addMovie(title, year);
    };
    return Controller;
}());
var controller = new Controller();
```

On the execution side, at loading time, the HTML page would look like it does in the following screenshot:

Model-view-controller at loading point

Then, if you use the form and add a movie, it'll automatically impact the view and display the new movie:

Model-view-controller after using the form

Model-view-controller limitations for the frontend

So, why is the model-view-controller pattern not that widely used when it comes to frontend programming supported by frameworks such as Angular? First, if you are using Angular for an app that provides a service, you are likely to have a backend with which you exchange some sort of information. Then, if your backend also uses the model-view-controller design pattern, you'll end up with the following hierarchy:

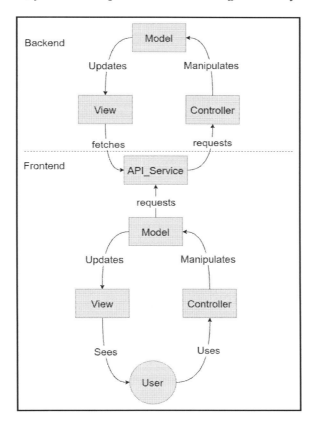

Model-view-controller frontend and backend

In this hierarchy, we have an MVC implementation on top of another MVC implementation. The implementations communicate with each other via an API service that sends requests to the backend controller and parses the resultant view. As a concrete example, if your user has to sign in to your app, they'll see the `signin` view on the frontend, which is powered by a `user` model and a `signin` controller. Once all of the information (email address, password) has been entered, the user clicks on the signin button. This click triggers a model update and the model then triggers an API call using the API service. The API service makes a request to the "user/signin" endpoint of your API. On the backend, the request is received by the `user` controller and forwarded to the `user` model. The backend `user` model will query your database to see if there is a matching user with the provided email address and password. Finally, a view will be output, containing the user information if the login was successful. Going back on the frontend, the API service will parse the produced view and return the relevant information to the frontend `user` model. In turn, the frontend `user` model will update the frontend `view`.

For some developers, that many layers and the fact that the architecture is kind of duplicated on the frontend and the backend just feels wrong, even though it brings maintainability through a well-defined separation-of-concerns.

The dual model-view-controller isn't the only concern. Another problem is that the frontend models will not be *pure* models as they must account for variables regarding the UI itself such as visible tab, forms validity, and so on. Hence, your frontend models tend to become hideous blobs of code where UI variables rub shoulders with the actual representation of your user.

Now, as always, you can avoid these traps and harness the advantages of the MVC pattern. Let's see how in the next section.

Angular's model-view-controller

In this section, I present an architecture for the MVC in Angular that proved itself. I used this architecture for the past 18 months at `toolwatch.io` (web, Android, and iOS). Obviously, the features we propose on the web version or on the mobile apps are the same and work in the same way. What changes are the views and the navigation schema.

The following diagram represents the overall architecture:

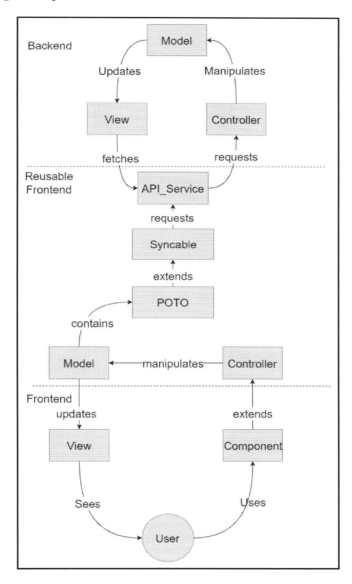

MVC for Angular

From top to bottom, we have the backend, the reusable pieces of the frontend, and the specialized frontend (mobile or web). As you can see, on the backend, nothing changes. We kept our classical MVC. Note that the frontend parts would work also with a non-MVC backend.

Our model will use that service to get, put, and delete a plain TypeScript object from the remote database through a hypothetical; JSON API.

Here's what our `user` TypeScript object looks like:

```typescript
class User {
    public constructor(private _email:string, private _password:string){}

    get email():string{
        return this._password;
    }

    get password():string{
        return this._email;
    }

    set email(email:string){
        this._password = email;
    }

    set password(password:string){
        this._email = password;
    }
}
```

Nothing too fancy here; only a plain TypeScript object that contains two attributes: `email:_string` and `password:_string`. These two attributes are initialized in the constructor using the TypeScript inline declaration style. We also leverage the getter/setter of TypeScript in order to access the `_password:string` and `_email:string` attributes. You might have noticed that the TypeScript getters/setters look like C# properties. Well, Microsoft is one of the principal industrial investigators for TypeScript, so it makes sense.

I do like the conciseness of the writing, especially when combined with the inline attribute declaration in the constructor. What I don't like, however, is the necessity for underscored variables names. The problem is that, once again, this TypeScript will be transpiled to JavaScript, and in JavaScript, variables and functions are a bit more abstract than, let's say, Java or C#.

Indeed, in our current example, we could invoke the getter of the User class as follows:

```
user:User = new User('mathieu.nayrolles@gmail.com', 'password');

console.log(user.email); // will print mathieu.nayrolles@gmail.com
```

As you can see, TypeScript doesn't care about the type of the target it's calling. It can be a variable named email or a function named email(). Either way, it works. The underlying rationale behind these odd behaviors, for an object-oriented programmer that is that in JavaScript, is that it's acceptable to do the following:

```
var email = function(){
    return "mathieu.nayrolles@gmail.com";
}
console.log(email);
```

Consequently, we need to differentiate the actual variables of the function with different names, hence the _.

Let's go back to our MVC implementation now that we have a fool-proof user object to manipulate. Now, we can have a user model that manipulates the user POTO (plain old TypeScript object) and the necessary variable for the graphical interface:

```
import { User } from '../poto/user';
import { APIService } from '../services/api.service';

export class UserModel{
    private user:User;
    private _loading:boolean = false;

    public constructor(private api:APIService){}

    public signin(email:string, password:string){

        this._loading = true;

        this.api.getUser(email, password).then(

            user => {
                this.user = user;
                this._loading = false;
            }
        );
    }

    public signup(email:string, password:string){
```

```
        this._loading = true;
        this.api.postUser(email, password).then(
            user => {
                this.user = user;
                this._loading = false;
            }
        );
    }

    get loading():boolean{
        return this._loading;
    }

}
```

Our model, named `UserModel`, receives an injection of an `APIService`. The implementation of the `APIService` is left to the reader as an exercise. In addition to the `APIService`, the `UserModel` owns the `user:User` and `loading:bool` attributes. The `user:User` represents the actual user with its password and email address. The `loading:bool`, however, will be used to determine whether or not a loading spinner should be visible in the view. As you can see, the `UserModel` defines the `signin` and `signup` methods. In these methods, we call the `getUser` and `postUser` methods of the `APIService`, which both take a user in an argument and return a promise containing said user that's been synchronized via the JSON API. On reception of these promises, we turn off the `loading:bool` spinner.

Here's the `APIService`:

```
import { Injectable } from '@angular/core';
import { Http }  from '@angular/http';
import { User } from '../poto/user';
import { Observable } from 'rxjs/Rx';
import 'rxjs/Rx';
import { resolve } from 'dns';
import { reject } from 'q';

@Injectable()
export class APIService {

  private userURL:string = "assets/users.json";

  constructor(private http: Http) { }

  /**
   * Return a Promise to a USer matching id
   * @param  {string}          email
```

```
 * @param   {string}            password
 * @return {Promise<User>}
 */
public getUser(email:string, password:string):Promise<User>{
    console.log('getUser', email, password);

        return this.http.get(this.userURL)
        /**
         * Transforms the result of the http get, which is observable
         * into one observable by item.
         */
        .flatMap(res => res.json().users)
        /**
         * Filters users by their email & password
         */
        .filter((user:any)=>{
            console.log("filter", user);
            return (user.email === email && user.password == password)
        })
        .toPromise()
        /**
         * Map the json user item to the User model
         */
        .then((user:any) => {
            console.log("map", user);
            return new User(
                email,
                password
            )
        });
}


  /**
   * Post an user Promise to a User
   * @param   {string}            email
   * @param   {string}            password
   * @return {Promise<User>}
   */
public postUser(email:string, password:string):Promise<User>{
    return new Promise<User>((resolve, reject) => {
        resolve(new User(
            email,
            password
        ));
    });
}


}
```

The `APIService` makes HTTP calls to parse a local JSON file containing the user:

```
{
    "users":[{
        "email":"mathieu.nayrolles@gmail.com",
        "password":"password"
    }]
}
```

`getUser(email:string, password:string):Promise<User>` and `postUser(email:string, password:string):Promise<User>` are using promises, just like we showed you in the previous chapter.

Then, there is the controller, which will also be a component in an Angular environment, as Angular components control the view that is displayed and so on:

```
@Component({
    templateUrl: 'user.html'
})
export class UserComponent{

    private model:UserModel;

    public UserComponent(api:APIService){

        this.model = new UserModel(api);
    }


    public signinClick(email:string, password:string){
        this.model.signin(email, password);
    }

    public signupClick(email:string, password:string){
        this.model.signup(email, password);
    }

}
```

As you can see, the controller (component) is really simple. We only have a reference to the model and we receive an injected `APIService` to be transfered to the model. Then, we have the `signinClick` and `signupClick` methods which receive user input from the view and transfer them to the model. The last piece, the view, looks like this:

```
<h1>Signin</h1>

<form action="#" onsubmit="signinClick(this.email.value,
```

```
this.password.value); return false;">

    email: <input name="email" type="text" id="email">
    password: <input name="password" type="password" id="password">
  <input [hidden]="model.loading" type="submit">
  <i [hidden]="!model.loading" class="fa fa-spinner" aria-
hidden="true"></i>
 </form>

 <h1>Signup</h1>

 <form action="#" onsubmit="signupClick(this.email.value,
this.password.value); return false;">

    email: <input name="email" type="text" id="email">
    password: <input name="password" type="password" id="password">
  <input [hidden]="model.loading" type="submit">
  <i [hidden]="!model.loading" class="fa fa-spinner" aria-
hidden="true"></i>
 </form>
```

Here, we have two forms: one for the signin and one for the signup. The forms are alike except for the onsubmit method they use. The signin form uses the signinClick method of our controller and the signup form uses the signupClick method. In addition to these two forms, we also have, on each form, a *font awesome* spinner that is only visible when the user model is *loading*. We achieve this by using the [hidden] Angular directive: [hidden]="!model.loading". Similarly, the submit buttons are hidden when the model is loading.

So, here it is, a functional MVC applied to Angular.

As I said at the beginning of this section, for me, the true usefulness of the MVC pattern in Angular comes from its extensibility. Indeed, leveraging the object-oriented aspect (and what comes with it) of TypeScript allows us to specialize controllers and models for different Angular applications. For example, if you have an Angular website and an Angular mobile application, as I do with toolwatch.io, then you have business logic you can use on both sides. It would be a shame to have two signins, two signups, and two of everything to code and maintain over time when we could have only one!

At toolwatch.io, for example, the web application uses standard Angular and we built the mobile applications using Ionic and Angular. Obviously, we have a lot of frontend logic shared between the mobile apps (Android and iOS) and the website. Ultimately, they tend to achieve the same purposes and functionalities. The only difference is the medium that's being used to utilize those functionalities.

In the following diagram, I loosely represent a more complete way of leveraging the MVC pattern with a focus on reusability and extensibility:

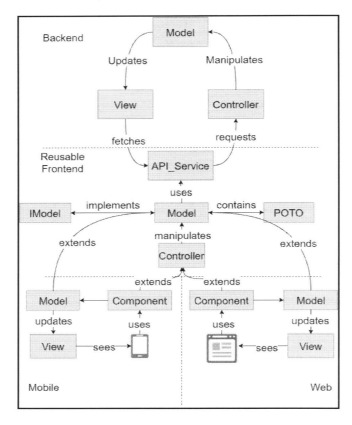

MVC for Angular

Once again, the backend stays as is. We have the same MVC pattern there. As a reminder, the MVC pattern on the backend is entirely up to you, and you could take advantage of the frontend MVC pattern with a functional Go backend, for example. What differs from the previous version of the MVC exposed here is the introduction of the *Reusable Frontend* part. In this part, we still have an API service in charge of consuming our JSON API. Then, we have a model that implements the IModel interface:

```
export interface IModel{

    protected get(POTO):POTO;
    protected put(POTO):POTO;
    protected post(POTO):POTO;
```

```
    protected delete(POTO):boolean;
    protected patch(POTO):POTO;


}
```

This interface defines the `put`, `post`, `delete`, and `patch` methods that have to be implemented in the subsequent models. The `POTO` type that these methods take as parameters and return is the mother class for any domain model you have in your program. A domain model represents a synchronizable entity of your business logic such as the `User` we used before. The domain model and the model part of the model-view-controller are not to be confused. They are not the same thing at all. In this architecture, `User` would expend `POTO`.

The model (of model-view-controller this time) contains a `POTO` in addition to implementing the `IModel` interface. It also contains the variables and methods you need to update your views. The implementation of the model itself is rather straightforward, as I showed earlier in this section. However, we can kick things up a notch by leveraging the generic aspect of TypeScript and envision the following:

```
export class AbstractModel<T extends POTO> implements IModel{
    protected T domainModel;

    public AbstractModel(protected api:APIService){}

    protected get(POTO):T{
        //this.api.get ...
    };
    protected put(T):T{
        //this.api.put...
    };
    protected post(T):T{
        //this.api.post...
    };
    protected delete(T):boolean{
        //this.api.delete...
    };
    protected patch(T):T{
        //this.api.patch...
    };
}

export class UserModel extends AbstractModel<User>{

    public AbstractModel(api:APIService){
        super(api);
    }
```

```
    public signin(email:string, password:string){

        this._loading = true;

        this.get(new User(email, password)).then(

            user => {
                this.user = user;
                this._loading = false;
            }
        );
    }

    public signup(email:string, password:string){

        this._loading = true;
        this.post(new User(email, password)).then(
            user => {
                this.user = user;
                this._loading = false;
            }
        );
    }
    //Only the code specialized for the UI !
}
```

Here, we have a generic `AbstractModel` that is constrained by `POTO`. This means that the actual instance of the `AbstractModel` generic class (known as a template in languages such as C++) is constrained to have a class specializing `POTO`. In other words, only domain models such as `User` can be used. So far, the separation of concern is excellent as well as its reusability. The last piece of the reusable part is the controller. In our signup/signin example, it would look very much like this:

```
export class UserController{

    public UserComponent(protected model:UserModel){
    }

    public signin(email:string, password:string){
        this.model.signin(email, password);
    }

    public signup(email:string, password:string){
        this.model.signup(email, password);
    }

}
```

Now, why do we need an additional building block here, and why can't we use a simple Angular component as we did for the simpler version of the Angular model-view-controller? Well, the thing is that, depending on what you use on top of your Angular core (Ionic, Meteor, and so on), the component isn't necessarily the main building block. For example, in the Ionic2 world, you use `Pages`, which are their custom version of the classical component.

So, for example, the mobile part would look like this:

```
export class LoginPage extends UserController{

    public LoginPage(api:APIService){
        super(new UserModel(api));
    }

    //Only what's different on mobile !

}
```

If need be, you can also extend `UserModel` and add some specialization, as shown in the preceding diagram. On the browser side:

```
@Component({
    templateUrl: 'login.html'
})
export class LoginComponent extends UserController{

    public UserComponent(api:APIService){

        super(new UserModel(api));
    }

    //Only what's different on browser !

}
```

Once again, you can also extend `UserModel` and add some specialization. The only remaining block to cover is the view. To my despair, there is no way to use extends or a style file for that. Hence, we are doomed to have duplication of HTML files between clients unless the HTML file is exactly the same between the mobile app and the browser app. From experience, this doesn't happen very often.

The whole reusable frontend can be shipped as a Git submodule, a standalone library, or as an `NgModule`. I personally use the git submodule approach as it allows me to have two separate repositories while enjoying auto-refresh on the client I am working on when I perform a modification on the shared frontend.

Note that this model-view-controller also works if you have several frontends hitting the same backend instead of several types of frontends. For example, in an e-commerce setup, you may want to have differently branded websites to sell different products that are all managed in the same backend, like what's possible with Magento's views.

Redux

Redux is a pattern that allows you to manage your event and application states in a safe way. It allows you to make sure that your application-wide states, resulting from navigation events or not, are managed in a single, non-accessible place.

Usually, the states of your application are stored in a TypeScript interface. Following the example we used in the previous section, we will implement login/logout functionalities for a user using a custom `APIService` that consumes JSON. In our case, the application has only one state: `logged`. Consequently, the interface would look like this:

```
export interface IAppState {
    logged: boolean;
}
```

This interface only contains a single logged boolean. It might seem like overkill to have an interface for such a common variable, but you'll find it handy when your applications start to grow. The state of our application can only be manipulated through `Action`. Actions are a type of event within the redux framework that are triggered and intercepted by a `Reducer`. The `Reducer` intercepts the actions and manipulates the state of our application. The `Reducer` is the only place where changes in state can happen.

Now that we have had a quick overview of the redux pattern, it's time to dive into its implementation. First, we will need to create a new Angular project and install the required packages:

- **ng new ng-redux**
- **cd ng-redux**
- **npm install – save redux @angular-redux/store**

Next, we will create our actions. As a reminder, actions are triggered by the application and intercepted by the `reducer` in order to manipulate application states. In our application, we only have two actions, login and logout:

```
import { Injectable } from '@angular/core';
import { Action } from 'redux';
```

```
@Injectable()
export class LoginAction {
  static LOGIN = 'LOGIN';
  static LOGOUT = 'LOGOUT';

  loggin(): Action {
    return { type: LoginAction.LOGIN };
  }

  logout(): Action {
    return { type: LoginAction.LOGOUT };
  }
}
```

As we can see in the preceding code, the LoginAction class is an Angular service in the sense that it is injectable. Consequently, any one part of our architecture could receive a list of actions through the automated dependency injection mechanisms of Angular that were presented in the previous chapter. Another thing to note is that our two actions are returning, well, Actions. The action class is composed of a type field, and we use static string variables to populate them.

The next item on the list is the reducer, which intercepts triggered actions and manipulates the states of our application accordingly. The reducer can be implemented as follows:

```
import { Action } from 'redux';
import { LoginAction } from './app.actions';

export interface IAppState {
    logged: boolean;
}

export const INITIAL_STATE: IAppState = {
  logged: false,
};

export function rootReducer(lastState: IAppState, action: Action):
IAppState {
  switch(action.type) {
    case LoginAction.LOGIN: return { logged: !lastState.logged };
    case LoginAction.LOGOUT: return { logged: !lastState.logged };
  }

  // We don't care about any other actions right now.
  return lastState;
}
```

For now, our reducer only manages two actions: login and logout. On reception of an action, we check the action type with a switch statement and simply reverse the value of the logged state. Because of our interface, this is the only place where we can modify the application states. At first sight, it can be perceived as a bottleneck and a poor separation of concerns. Now, the bottleneck part, in the sense that all happens there, is by design. The main idea behind Redux is that complex stateful JavaScript applications are hard to manage, because the states of the application can change in multiple ways. For example, an asynchronous call and a navigation event can both change the overall states of the application in subtle and hard-to-debug ways. Here, using the Redux functionalities, everything is managed in the same place. For the separation of concerns argument, which is very much valid, nothing prevents us from manipulating the state (for example, return { logged: !lastState.logged }; in our case) in well-named, loosely coupled functions.

Now that our store, Redux, and actions are implemented, we can start to manipulate them inside our component:

```
import { Component, OnDestroy } from '@angular/core';

import { NgRedux } from '@angular-redux/store';
import { LoginAction } from './app.actions';
import { IAppState } from "./store";
import { APIService } from './api.service';

@Component({
  selector: 'app-root',
  templateUrl: './app.component.html',
  styleUrls: ['./app.component.css']
})
export class AppComponent implements OnDestroy {
  title = 'app';
  subscription;
  logged: boolean;

  constructor(
    private ngRedux: NgRedux<IAppState>,
    private api:APIService) {

      this.subscription = ngRedux.select<boolean>('logged')
      .subscribe(logged => this.logged = logged);
    }

  login(email:string, password:string) {
    this.api.login(email, password);
  }

  logout() {
```

```
      this.api.logout();
   }

  ngOnDestroy() {
    this.subscription.unsubscribe();
  }
}
```

A lot is happening here. Let's break it down piece by piece. First, there's the constructor:

```
constructor(
    private ngRedux: NgRedux<IAppState>,
    private api:APIService) {

      this.subscription = ngRedux.select<boolean>('logged')
      .subscribe(logged => this.logged = logged);
    }
```

In this constructor, we expect to receive an injection of NgRedux<IAppState> that manipulates our state and the APIService that is slightly modified from the previous section to accommodate our new pattern. Inside the constructor, we have the ngRedux.select<boolean>('logged') instruction, which allow us to access an observable of the logged variables from the IAppState interface. As you can see, by design, it's not possible to change the value of logged here, as you can only obtain an observable to it. Being an observable, we can subscribe to it and define a component when its value changes. In our case, we affect the value of the logged class member to the new value of the logged state.

Next comes the login and logout methods that serve as proxies to the ApiService calls:

```
login(email:string, password:string) {
    this.api.login(email, password);
  }

logout() {
    this.api.logout();
  }
```

Finally, we can see the implementation of the ngOnDestroy function made mandatory by implementing the OnDestroy interface. While not obligatory, the ngOnDestroy function unsubscribes from the logged observer, which will save us a few milliseconds if the logged state changes and the component does not exist anymore:

```
ngOnDestroy() {
    this.subscription.unsubscribe();
  }
```

Let's have a look at the HTML that's linked to our component. It is fairly simple and only displays the value of the logged state and two buttons that, you've guessed it, allow us to log in and out of our application:

```
<div style="text-align:center">
  <p>{{logged}}</p>
  <button (click)="login('foo', 'bar')">Login</button>
  <button (click)="logout()">Logout</button>
</div>
```

Here's what it looks like:

The next item on the list is the modification of the `APIService` so that it uses our new patterns instead of the MVC:

```
import { Injectable } from '@angular/core';
import { Http }  from '@angular/http';
import { User } from './user';
import 'rxjs/Rx';
import { NgRedux } from '@angular-redux/store';
import { LoginAction } from './app.actions';
import {IAppState } from './store';

@Injectable()
export class APIService {

  private userURL:string = "assets/users.json";

  constructor(
      private http: Http,
      private ngRedux: NgRedux<IAppState>,
      private actions: LoginAction) { }

  /**
   * Return a Promise to a USer matching id
   * @param  {string}          email
   * @param  {string}          password
   * @return {Promise<User>}
   */
```

```
public login(email:string, password:string){
    console.log('login', email, password);

    this.http.get(this.userURL)
    /**
     * Transforms the result of the http get, which is observable
     * into one observable by item.
     */
    .flatMap(res => res.json().users)
    /**
     * Filters users by their email & password
     */
    .filter((user:any)=>{
        console.log("filter", user);
        return (user.email === email && user.password == password)
    })
    .toPromise()
    /**
     * Map the json user item to the User model
     */
    .then((user:any) => {
        console.log("map", user);
        this.ngRedux.dispatch(this.actions.loggin());
    });
}

/**
 * Logout a User
 */
public logout(){
    this.ngRedux.dispatch(this.actions.logout());
}

}
```

In this version, we use the same technique except we do not return promises anymore. Indeed, in this version, we simply dispatch actions to our reducer with the following:

```
this.ngRedux.dispatch(this.actions.loggin());
```

And:

```
this.ngRedux.dispatch(this.actions.logout());
```

Once again, the modification of the state is indirect; we simply dispatch an action that will be caught by the reducer rather than manipulate the state. In other words, it's safe and centralized to a single point.

Finally, we need to adjust the main app module to reflect all our changes:

```
import { BrowserModule } from '@angular/platform-browser';
import { NgModule } from '@angular/core';
import { HttpModule } from '@angular/http';

import { NgReduxModule, NgRedux } from '@angular-redux/store';
import { AppComponent } from './app.component';

import { rootReducer, IAppState, INITIAL_STATE } from './store';
import { LoginAction } from './app.actions';
import { APIService } from './api.service';

@NgModule({
  declarations: [
    AppComponent
  ],
  imports: [
    NgReduxModule,
    HttpModule,
  ],
  providers: [APIService, LoginAction],
  bootstrap: [AppComponent]
})
export class AppModule {

  constructor(ngRedux: NgRedux<IAppState>) {
    // Tell @angular-redux/store about our rootReducer and our initial
state.
    // It will use this to create a redux store for us and wire up all the
    // events.
    ngRedux.configureStore(
      rootReducer,
      INITIAL_STATE);
  }
}
```

We first imported the NgRedux module and the HttpModule, which will be used in the application. Then, the constructor of the AppModule will receive an injected NgRedux instance and configure our Redux store. The store also receives a default state that we initialized earlier.

Summary

In this chapter, we saw two patterns: Redux and MVC. Redux and the MVC can be used to achieve the same purposes (manage the states of our application in reaction to asynchronous events or user actions). Both patterns have advantages and shortcomings. The advantages of the MVC in the Angular application, from my point of view, is that everything is well defined and separated. Indeed, we have a domain object (`User`), a model (`UserModel`), and a view linked to a component. We saw that same model and domain object across many components and views in favor of reuse across apps. The problem is that it can get expensive to create new functionalities in our apps because you'll have to create—or, at least, modify,—a good chunk of architecture.

Additionally, whether by mistake or by design, if you share models across several components and services, it can be extremely painful to identify and eradicate the source of a bug. The Redux pattern is more recent and, most of all, more adapted to the JavaScript ecosystem, as it has been created for it. It's relatively easy to add functionalities in terms of state in our applications and to manipulate them in a safe way. From experience, I can assure you that bugs that entire teams are mystified by for days are much less frequent when using the Redux patterns. However, the separation of concerns within the application is less clear and you can end up with a thousand lines of Redux in the most complex application. Sure, we can create several reducers in addition to the root one, separate our stores with big functionalities, and create helper functions to manipulate our states. As it's not imposed by the patterns, more often than not, I found myself reviewing enormous reducers that are costly to refactor.

In the next chapter, we will investigate stability patterns for our Angular application, which will ensure that our applications continue to be usable when all odds are stacked against us.

5

Stability Patterns

Stability is one of the cornerstones of software engineering. No matter what, you must expect the worst from your environment and your users and be prepared for it. Your Angular applications should be able to operate in a degraded mode when your backend is burning and smoothly recover when it comes back online.

In this chapter, we will learn about stability patterns and anti-patterns, such as the following:

- Timeouts
- Circuit breaker
- Factory
- Memento
- The prototype and reusable pool

Timeouts

In the previous chapters, we experimented with API services with the intent of consuming APIs of any type of content that were created by our hypothetical backend. If I had to share a one-liner about what I learned during my online adventures, it would be *don't trust anybody...especially not yourself*. What I mean by that is that you can never trust an API to work as expected, even if it is your own API. You should always expect everything that can go wrong to, well, go wrong. One of the less harmful things that can happen when trying to communicate with your backend is that it won't respond. While this one-way communication is harmless for your Angular applications, it is most frustrating for your users. In this recipe, we will learn how to implement timeouts in our external call and how to react to unresponsive APIs.

Fortunately, there is a very simple way to prevent our user from getting frustrated about unresponsive APIs: timeouts. A timeout is a simple defense mechanism that allows your application to wait a fixed amount of time and not a millisecond more. Let's create a new project to test it out:

```
ng new timeout
cd timeout
ng g service API
```

This will create a new project and a service called API. At first glance, there is not much to look at:

```
import { Injectable } from '@angular/core';

@Injectable()
export class ApiService {

  constructor() { }

}
```

We will need to add the HttpClient component in app.module.ts as follows:

```
import { BrowserModule } from '@angular/platform-browser';
import { NgModule } from '@angular/core';
import { HttpClientModule } from '@angular/common/http';

import { AppComponent } from './app.component';
import { ApiService } from './api.service';

@NgModule({
  declarations: [
    AppComponent
  ],
  imports: [
    BrowserModule,
    HttpClientModule
  ],
  providers: [ApiService],
  bootstrap: [AppComponent]
})
export class AppModule { }
```

Then, we want to inject the HttpClient component into our API service client in order to have access to its methods:

```
import { Injectable } from '@angular/core';
import { HttpClient } from '@angular/common/http';
```

```
@Injectable()
export class ApiService {

  constructor(private http:HttpClient) { }

}
```

We will add a new method in our `APIService` that simply makes an `http.get` to the GitHub repository that contains the code for this book(`https://github.com/MathieuNls/Angular-Design-Patterns-and-Best-Practices`):

```
import { Injectable } from '@angular/core';
import { HttpClient } from '@angular/common/http';

@Injectable()
export class ApiService {

  constructor(private http: HttpClient) { }

  public getURL(url: string): void {
    this.http.get(url)
    .subscribe(data => {
      console.log(data);
    });
  }

}
```

This is followed by an injection of `ApiService` and a call to the new `getURL` method in the `AppComponent`:

```
import { Component } from '@angular/core';
import { ApiService } from './api.service';

@Component({
  selector: 'app-root',
  templateUrl: './app.component.html',
  styleUrls: ['./app.component.css']
})
export class AppComponent {
  title = 'app';

  constructor(private api: ApiService){
api.getURL("https://github.com/MathieuNls/Angular-Design-Patterns-and-Best-
Practices")
  }
}
```

Now, if we were to execute this, we would have a gracious HTTP response, and the HTML of the web page would be printed out in the console. The problem, however, is that we have no countermeasure in place in the case that github.com is down and does not respond:

```
import { Injectable } from '@angular/core';
import { HttpClient } from '@angular/common/http';

@Injectable()
export class ApiService {

  constructor(private http: HttpClient) { }

  public getURL(url: string): void {

    let timeout;

    let sub = this.http.get(url)
      .subscribe((res) => {
        console.log(res);
        clearTimeout(timeout)
      });

    timeout = setTimeout(
      () => { sub.unsubscribe() }, 1000
    );
  }

}
```

In this version of the getURL function, we must first declare a timeout variable that will contain a NodeJS timeout. Then, instead of performing a regular HTTP.get, we will subscribe to the response. Finally, after the subscription to the result, we assign the timeout variable with the setTimeout function. We use this function to unsubscribe from the response after 1,000 ms. Consequently, we only wait one second for the http reply. If the reply does not arrive within that time, we automatically unsubscribe and allow our application to continue. Of course, our users will have to be warned in some way that the operation was unsuccessful.

Circuit breaker

The timeout pattern we implemented in the previous section is efficient at protecting the patience of our users and, ultimately, our Angular application. However, in the case that the API is not responding because something went wrong on the server side, let's say 80% of your server is down and the remaining 20% is trying to manage the load, your clients will most likely repeatedly retry the action that timed out. Consequently, this puts even more stress on our dying backend infrastructure.

A circuit is an automatic device for stopping the flow of the current in an electric circuit as a safety measure. Circuit breakers are used to detect failures and encapsulate the logic of preventing a failure from reoccurring constantly (during maintenance, temporary external system failure, or unexpected system difficulties).

Concretely, within the framework of an Angular app, a circuit breaker will prevent the client from performing API requests when there are too many failures. After a given amount of time, the circuit will allow some of the queries to go through and consume the API. If these queries return without any problems, then the circuit will close itself and allow all the requests to go through:

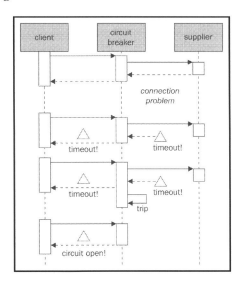

In the preceding diagram, we can see how the circuit breaker operates. All requests go through the circuit breaker, and if the supplier answers the requests in time, the circuit stays closed. When problems start to occur, the circuit breaker notices, and if enough requests timeout, then the circuit opens and prevents requests from going through.

Finally, after a given amount of time, the circuit breaker tries to resend requests to the supplier:

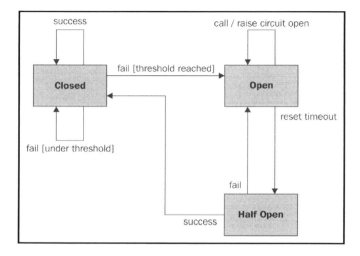

From an implementation point of view, we will need the `ApiStatus` and `Call` classes, which are responsible for keeping track of the call we make to diverse APIs:

```
//ApiStatus class
class ApiStatus {

  public lastFail: number
  public calls: Call[]

  constructor(public url: string) { }

  //Compute the fail percentage
  public failPercentage(timeWindow: number): number {

    var i = this.calls.length - 1;
    var success = 0
    var fail = 0;

    while (this.calls[i].time > Date.now() - timeWindow && i >= 0) {
      if (this.calls[i].status) {
        success++;
      } else {
        fail++;
      }
    i--;
    }
```

```
        return fail / (fail + success)
    }

}
```

The `APIStatus` contains the statistics for the on root api. We take into account that we might use several APIs in our application. Each API has to be linked to its own circuit breaker. First, we have the `lastFail` variable, which contains the date at which the last call to this API failed. Then, we have a `calls` array that contains all the calls made to a given API. In addition to the constructor that defines the URL property, we have the `failPercentage` function. This function is responsible for computing the percentage of calls that failed within the `timeWindows` time. To do this, we iterate over all the calls in a reverse chronological order until we reach $Date.now() - timeWindow$ or the end of the `calls` array. Within the `while` loop, we increment two number variables called `success` and `fail` with regard to the status of the current call. At the end, we return the percentage of failed calls. This percentage will be used to determine the status of the circuit breaker.

The `Call` class is rather simple:

```
//An Api Call
class Call {
    constructor(public time: number, public status: boolean) { }
}
```

It only contains two properties: time and status. We are now ready to implement an API client for our *Angular* app that implements a circuit breaker. First, we have to create the class:

```
import { Injectable } from '@angular/core';
import { HttpClient } from '@angular/common/http';

@Injectable()
export class ApiwithBreakerService {

    constructor(private http: HttpClient) { }
```

Then, we have to add the property for `ApiwithBreakerService`:

```
private apis: Map<string, ApiStatus>;
private failPercentage: number = 0.2;
private timeWindow : number = 60*60*24;
private timeToRetry : number = 60;
```

These properties will allow us to implement the circuit breaker pattern. First, we have a map of `string`, an `ApiStatus` that is used to store the API status of many APIs. Then, we have `failPercentage`, which defines how many calls can fail, as a percentage, before we open the circuit. The `timeWindow` variable defines the amount of time that is used to compute `failPercentage`. Here, we have a maximum of 20% of calls that can fail within a 24-hour window before we open this circuit and prevent other calls from being made. Finally, we have `timeToRetry`, which states how long we have to wait before trying to reclose the circuit.

Here is the modified `getURL` function from the timeout section:

```
//Http get an url
public getURL(url: string): void {

  var rootUrl = this.extractRootDomain(url);

  if(this.isClosed(rootUrl) || this.readyToRetry(rootUrl)){
    let timeout;

    let sub = this.http.get(url)
      .subscribe((res) => {
        console.log(res);
        clearTimeout(timeout);
        this.addCall(rootUrl, true);
      });
    timeout = setTimeout(
      () => {
        sub.unsubscribe();
        this.addCall(rootUrl, false);
      }, 1000
    );
  }
}
```

We kept the same core functionalities from the previous section with the timeout, but we embedded it in an `if` statement:

```
if(this.isClosed(rootUrl) || this.readyToRetry(rootUrl))
```

The `if` statement checks if the circuit is closed or if we are ready to retry on an open circuit.

We also added calls to the `addCall` function:

```
//Add a call
private addCall(url: string, status: boolean) {

  let res = this.apis.get(url);

  if (res == null) {
    res = new ApiStatus(url);
    this.apis.set(url, res);
  }

  res.calls.push(new Call(Date.now(), status));

  if(!status){
    res.lastFail = Date.now();
  }
}
```

The `addCall` function adds a new call to an `ApiStatus` that's stored inside the `apis` map. It also updates the `lastFail` properties of the `ApiStatus` instance if the call was unsuccessful.

What remains are the `readyToRetry` and `isClosed` functions:

```
//Are we ready to retry
private readyToRetry(url:string): boolean {

  return this.apis.get(url).lastFail < (Date.now() - this.timeToRetry)
}

//Is it closed ?
private isClosed(url :string) : boolean {

  return this.apis.get(url) == null ||
    !(this.apis.get(url).failPercentage(this.timeWindow) >
this.failPercentage);
  }
```

In the `readyToRetry` function, we simply check that the latest fail is older than the time it is now minus `timeToRetry`. In the `isClosed` function, we check if the percentage of failed calls during the time window is greater than the maximum allowed. Here is the complete implementation:

```
import { Injectable } from '@angular/core';
import { HttpClient } from '@angular/common/http';
```

```
//ApiStatus class
class ApiStatus {

  public lastFail: number
  public calls: Call[]

  constructor(public url: string) { }

  //Compute the fail percentage
  public failPercentage(timeWindow: number): number {

    var i = this.calls.length - 1;
    var success = 0
    var fail = 0;

    while (this.calls[i].time > Date.now() - timeWindow && i >= 0) {
      if (this.calls[i].status) {
        success++;
      } else {
        fail++;
      }
      i--;
    }

    return fail / (fail + success)
  }

}

//An Api Call
class Call {
  constructor(public time: number, public status: boolean) { }
}

@Injectable()
export class ApiwithBreakerService {

  constructor(private http: HttpClient) { }

  private apis: Map<string, ApiStatus>;
  private failPercentage: number = 0.2;
  private timeWindow : number = 60*60*24;
  private timeToRetry : number = 60;

  //Http get an url
  public getURL(url: string): void {

    var rootUrl = this.extractRootDomain(url);
```

```
    if(this.isClosed(rootUrl) || this.readyToRetry(rootUrl)){
      let timeout;

      let sub = this.http.get(url)
        .subscribe((res) => {
          console.log(res);
          clearTimeout(timeout);
          this.addCall(rootUrl, true);
        });
      timeout = setTimeout(
        () => {
          sub.unsubscribe();
          this.addCall(rootUrl, false);
        }, 1000
      );
    }
  }

  //Add a call
  private addCall(url: string, status: boolean) {

    let res = this.apis.get(url);

    if (res == null) {
      res = new ApiStatus(url);
      this.apis.set(url, res);
    }

    res.calls.push(new Call(Date.now(), status));

    if(!status){
      res.lastFail = Date.now();
    }
  }

  //Are we ready to retry
  private readyToRetry(url:string): boolean {

    return this.apis.get(url).lastFail < (Date.now() - this.timeToRetry)
  }

  //Is it closed ?
  private isClosed(url :string) : boolean {

    return this.apis.get(url) == null ||
      !(this.apis.get(url).failPercentage(this.timeWindow) >
this.failPercentage);
  }
```

```
    private extractHostname(url: string) : string {
      var hostname;
      //find & remove protocol (http, ftp, etc.) and get hostname

      if (url.indexOf("://") > -1) {
        hostname = url.split('/')[2];
      }
      else {
        hostname = url.split('/')[0];
      }

      //find & remove port number
      hostname = hostname.split(':')[0];
      //find & remove "?"
      hostname = hostname.split('?')[0];

      return hostname;
    }

  private extractRootDomain(url: string) : string{
    var domain = this.extractHostname(url),
      splitArr = domain.split('.'),
      arrLen = splitArr.length;

    //extracting the root domain here
    //if there is a subdomain
    if (arrLen > 2) {
      domain = splitArr[arrLen - 2] + '.' + splitArr[arrLen - 1];
      //check to see if it's using a Country Code Top Level Domain (ccTLD)
(i.e. ".me.uk")
      if (splitArr[arrLen - 1].length == 2 && splitArr[arrLen - 1].length
== 2) {
        //this is using a ccTLD
        domain = splitArr[arrLen - 3] + '.' + domain;
      }
    }
    return domain;
  }
}
```

Note that we have two helper functions that do not directly participate in the implementation of the circuit patterns, only extracting the root URL of a call in order to compute a shared status by root APIs. Thanks to these helper functions, we can have `http://someapi.com/users` and `http://someapi.com/sales` share the same status while `http://anotherapi.com/someCall` has its own separated `ApiStatus`.

The timeout and the circuit breaker patterns work in parallel in order to reduce self-denial. Self-denial is the art of dooming your backend servers yourself. This tends to happen when you have an application behaving improperly and making thousands of calls per second to your backend architecture.

Factory

Let's assume that we have a `User` class with two private variables: `lastName:string` and `firstName:string`. In addition, this simple class proposes that the `hello` method prints `"Hi I am"`, `this.firstName`, `this.lastName`:

```
class User{
    constructor(private lastName:string, private firstName:string){
    }
    hello(){
        console.log("Hi I am", this.firstName, this.lastName);
    }
}
```

Now, consider that we receive users through a JSON API. It will more than likely look something like this:

```
[{"lastName":"Nayrolles","firstName":"Mathieu"}...].
```

With the following snippet, we can create a `User`:

```
let userFromJSONAPI: User =
JSON.parse('[{"lastName":"Nayrolles","firstName":"Mathieu"}]')[0];
```

Up until now, the TypeScript compiler hasn't complained, and it executes smoothly. It works because the parse method returns `any` (for example, the TypeScript equivalent of the Java object). Sure enough, we can convert the `any into User`. However, `userFromJSONAPI.hello();` will yield the following:

```
json.ts:19
 userFromJSONAPI.hello();
                 ^
 TypeError: userFromUJSONAPI.hello is not a function
     at Object.<anonymous> (json.ts:19:18)
     at Module._compile (module.js:541:32)
     at Object.loader (/usr/lib/node_modules/ts-node/src/ts-node.ts:225:14)
     at Module.load (module.js:458:32)
     at tryModuleLoad (module.js:417:12)
     at Function.Module._load (module.js:409:3)
```

```
    at Function.Module.runMain (module.js:575:10)
    at Object.<anonymous> (/usr/lib/node_modules/ts-node/src/bin/ts-
node.ts:110:12)
    at Module._compile (module.js:541:32)
    at Object.Module._extensions..js (module.js:550:10)
```

Why? Well, the left-hand side of assignation is defined as User, sure, but it'll be erased when we transpile it to JavaScript.

The type-safe TypeScript way to do it would be as follows:

```
let validUser =
JSON.parse('[{"lastName":"Nayrolles","firstName":"Mathieu"}]')
  .map((json: any):User => {
      return new User(json.lastName, json.firstName);
  })[0];
```

Interestingly enough, the typeof function won't help you either. In both cases, it'll display Object instead of User, as the very concept of User doesn't exist in JavaScript.

While the direct type-safe approach works, it isn't very expansible nor reusable. Indeed, the map callback method would have to be duplicated everywhere you receive a JSON user. The most convenient way to do that is through the Factory pattern. A Factory is used for objects without exposing the instantiation logic to the client.

If we were to have a factory to create a user, it would look like this:

```
export class POTOFactory{

    /**
     * Builds an User from json response
     * @param  {any}  jsonUser
     * @return {User}
     */
    static buildUser(jsonUser: any): User {

        return new User(
            jsonUser.firstName,
            jsonUser.lastName
        );
    }

}
```

Here, we have a static method named `buildUser` that receives a JSON object and takes all the required value inside the JSON object to invoke, with the right attributes, a hypothetical `User` constructor. The method is static, like all the methods of such a factory. Indeed, we don't need to save any states or instance-bound variables in a factory; we only encapsulate away the gruesome creation of users. Note that your factory will likely be shared for the rest of your POTOs.

Memento

The memento pattern is a really useful pattern in the context of Angular. In Angular-powered applications, we use and overuse two ways binding between domain models such as `User` or `Movie`.

Let's consider two components, one named `Dashboard` and the other one named `EditMovie`. On the `Dashboard` component, you have a list of movies displayed in the context of our IMDb-like application. The view of such a dashboard could look like this:

```
<div *ngFor="let movie of model.movies">
    <p>{{movie.title}}</p>
    <p>{{movie.year}}</p>
</div>
```

This simple view owns a `ngFor` directive that iterates over the list of movies contained in a model. Then, for each movie, it displays two `p` elements containing the title and the release year, respectively.

Now, the `EditMovie` components access one of the movies on the `model.movies` array and allow the user to edit it:

```
<form>
    <input id="title" name="title" type="text" [(ngModel)]="movie.title" />
    <input id="year" name="year" type="text" [(ngModel)]="movie.year" />
</form>

<a href="/back">Cancel</a>
```

Thanks to the two ways binding used here, the modifications performed on the movie title and year will directly impact the dashboard. As you can see, we have a cancel button here. While the user might expect that the modification is synchronized in real time, he also expects that the cancel button/link cancels the modifications that have been done on the movie.

That is where the Memento pattern comes into play. This pattern allows performing undo operations on objects. It can be implemented in many ways, but the simplest one is to go with cloning. Using cloning, we can store one version of our object, at a given moment, and, if need be, get back to it. Let's enhance our Movie object from the prototype pattern as follows:

```
export class Movie implements Prototype {

    private title:string;
    private year:number;
    //...


    public constructor()
    public constructor(title:string = undefined, year:number = undefined)
    {
        if(title == undefined || year == undefined){
            //do the expensive creation
        }else{
            this.title = title;
            this.year = year;
        }
    }

    clone() : Movie {
        return new Movie(this.title, this.year);
    }

    restore(movie:Movie){
        this.title = movie.title;
        this.year = movie.year;
    }
}
```

In this new version, we added the restore(movie:Movie) method, which takes a Movie as an argument and affects the local attributes to the values of the received movie.

Then, in practice, the constructor of our `EditMovie` component could look like this:

```
private memento:Movie;

constructor(private movie:Movie){

    this.memento = movie.clone();
}

public cancel(){
    this.movie.restore(this.memento);
}
```

What's interesting is that you are not limited to one memento over time, as you can have as many as you want.

Summary

In this chapter, we saw patterns that aim to improve the stability of our Angular applications. It is worth noting that most of the aim, in fact, is for protecting our backend infrastructures from overheating. Indeed, the timeout and the circuit breaker, when combined, allow us to give our backends a break while they come back online. In addition, the memento and the reusable pool aim to keep the client-side information we could have re-requested from the backend if we were not to store them.

In the next chapter, we will cover performance patterns and best practices to improve the speed at which our application operates.

6
Performance Patterns

In the previous chapter, we investigated stability patterns. Stability patterns are here for your application so that it can survive bugs. It is ludicrous to expect applications to be shipped without any bugs, and trying to achieve this will wear your team out. Instead, we learned how to live with it and made sure that our application is resilient enough to live through bugs. In this chapter, we will focus on performance patterns and anti-patterns. These patterns define architectures and practices that significantly affect the performance of your application in a positive or negative way.

In detail, we will learn about the following:

- AJAX overkill
- Unbound result sets
- Proxy
- Filters and Pipes
- Loops
- Change detection
- Immutability
- Prototype and the reusable pool

AJAX overkill

If your application is a bit more than a throwaway prototype or a glorified one-pager, you are likely dealing with remote APIs. These remotes APIs, in turn, are communicating with a backend layer (for example, PHP, Ruby, or Golang) and databases (for example, MySQL, MS SQL, or Oracle).

While this book focuses on *Angular* application, we cannot ignore the fact that they do not usually exist by themselves. Indeed, any meaningful application will need to pull and push data from/to somewhere.

With that in mind, let's imagine that your application is some sort of frontend for an online e-commerce site such as Amazon. This made-up application would certainly have a profile page where your users can see their past and ongoing commands.

Let's further specify our application by imagining that your APIs, endpoints are specified as follows:

```
GET /orders
```

This returns the orders of logged-in users.

Here is an example of a JSON return call:

```json
{
  "orders":[
    {
     "id":"123",
     "date": "10/10/10",
     "amount": 299,
     "currency": "USD"
    },
    {
     "id":"321",
     "date": "11/11/11",
     "amount": 1228,
     "currency": "USD"
    },
    {
     "id":"322",
     "date": "11/12/11",
     "amount": 513,
     "currency": "USD"
     },

    . . .

  ]
}
```

For the sake of clarity and brevity, we will assume that our users are magically authenticated and that their authorization to access given API endpoints is magical as well.

For each command, you have access to a GET /command_details API where, for a given ID, you can retrieve the details of the command:

```json
{
  "items":[
    {
      "id":123,
      "qty":1,
      "price": 2,
      "tax_rate": 0.19,
      "currency": "USD",
      "shipped_at": "10/10/10",
      "received_at": "11/10/10"
    },
    {
      "id":124,
      "qty":2,
      "price": 3,
      "tax_rate": 0.19,
      "currency": "USD",
      "shipped_at": "10/10/10",
      "received_at": "11/10/10"
    }
    ...
  ]
}
```

The Angular side of things could be a simple expansion panel that's implemented using the expansion panel of the Google Material Design components suite as shown in the following screenshot:

We could also add a GET /items_details that returns the details of an item, but let's stop here for now.

Now, let's assume that every API call takes 100 ms to complete and another 10 ms for transforming the JSON into TypeScript objects. An experienced developer would certainly first fetch all the commands of the given user and pre-fetch the details of each command so that the user will not have to wait when a given panel is expanded. If our APIs can handle 100 requests per second, which is respectable, then we could only serve nine clients per second, assuming that they each have ten commands. Nine clients per second don't sound impressive...

Indeed, 10 clients hitting the *order resume* page at once will cost us 1/10 of our capacity and provoke an additional 100 calls (10 clients × 10 commands). Consequently, the 10th client will not be served during the first second. It may not sound that alarming, however, we are only talking about 10 users.

This effect is known as the AJAX overkill performance anti-pattern. As a frontend developer, I have access to APIs that fulfill my every need, and I use them to make my clients happy. However, pre loading every detail of every command, and potentially every detail of every item, is a terrible idea. You put unnecessary stress on your backend architecture on the off chance that your customer wants to access the details of the last commands immediately.

For the sake of your backend infrastructure, it might be worth it to only request the details of the commands when the user actually wants to see them.

This goes hand in hand with unbound APIs. Once again, the backend architecture is not within the scope of this book, however, if we were to talk about the performance of Angular applications, we would have to mention it. If you have control over the APIs you consume, then make sure that they expose some sort of pagination and that you use it properly.

Proxy patterns

Continuing our investigation into unbounded APIs and AJAX overkill, in the previous recipe, we established that both should be avoided, but the solution to this was to make APIs change in case the APIs were not paginated. This assumes that you have access to these APIs or to someone who has. While this is a reasonable assumption to make, it will not hold true in all cases.

What can we do, besides not making requests (obviously), to preserve those poorly designed and out-of-control APIs? Well, an elegant way to resolve this problem would be to use the proxy pattern. The proxy pattern is used to control access to an object. You surely know that the web proxy can control access to web pages given a user's credentials. In this recipe, we will not talk about the web proxy, but the objected-oriented proxy. In the object-oriented proxy, we do not control so much the access to the object regarding security, but regarding features.

As an example, an image manipulation software is to list and display high-resolution photo objects that are in a folder, but users will not always visualize all the images in the given folder. Consequently, some images will have been loaded for nothing.

How does that relate to our API problem, though? Using the proxy pattern, we can control at which time we actually want to perform our API request, while keeping our collection of commands neat and tidy. First, let's have a look at the proxy UML:

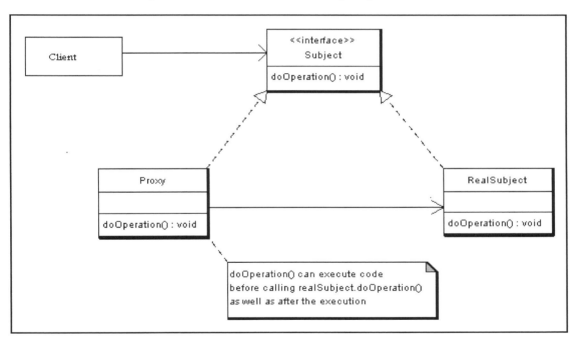

First, we have the `Subject` interface that defines the `doOperation()` method. This interface is implemented by the `Proxy` and `RealSubject` classes. The `Proxy` class contains a reference to a `realSubject` class, which will be populated at the right time. What could it look like for our purposes?

First, we have a simple interface named `OnlineCommand`:

```
import { Item } from "./item";
export interface OnlineCommand {
fetchItems() : Item[]
}
```

In this interface, the only method is defined: `fetchItems()`. This method returns the items contained in the command.

Then, our component has an array of commands that represent the commands of our customer:

```
import { Component } from '@angular/core';
import { OnlineCommand } from './online-command';

@Component({
    selector: 'app-root',
    templateUrl: './app.component.html',
    styleUrls: ['./app.component.css']
})
export class AppComponent {
title = 'app';
private commands:OnlineCommand[]
}
```

In this short component, we only have the commands of our customer in addition to what makes an Angular component a component.

For the HTML part, we simply iterate over the collection of commands and, on click, call the `fetchItems` function:

```
<ul>
  <li *ngFor="let item of commands; let i = index"
(click)="item.fetchItems()">
    {{i}} {{item}}
 </li>
</ul>
```

Then, we have the `RealCommand` class that implements the `OnlineCommand` interface:

```
import { OnlineCommand } from "./online-command";
import { Item } from "./item";

//RealCommand is a real command that has the right to do
//API calls
export class RealCommand implements OnlineCommand{

   public fetchItems() : Item[] {
       //This would come from an API call
       return [new Item(), new Item()];
   }
}
```

The last piece of the puzzle, albeit the most important one, is the proxyfied version of the online command:

```
import { OnlineCommand } from "./online-command";
import { RealCommand } from "./real-command";
import { Item } from "./item";

//A Proxified Command
export class ProxyfiedCommand implements OnlineCommand{
     //Reference to the real deal
     private real:RealCommand;

     //Constructor
     constructor() {
        this.real = new RealCommand();
     }
     //The Proxified fetchItems.
     //It only exists as a placeholder and if we need it
     //we' ll the real command.
     public fetchItems() : Item[] {
     console.log("About the call the API");
     let items = this.real.fetchItems();
     console.log("Called it");
     return items;
   }
}
```

As discussed previously, the proxyfied version of the online command contains a reference to a real command that, for all intents and purposes, is our actual command. The point here is that the costly operation is the feature we only want to access when we really need to. On the HTML side, everything is elegantly hidden behind the encapsulation. On the TypeScript side, we only perform the call when the user requests the details and not before.

Loop count

Web applications of any kind are often filled with loops. It could be a loop on products for *Amazon.com*, a loop on your transactions for your bank website, a loop on your phone calls for your phone carrier website, and so on. Worst of all, you can have many loops on a page. When these loops iterate over static collections, it sure takes time to process when the page is being generated, unless there is nothing you can do about it. You can still apply the patterns we saw earlier in this chapter to reduce your collection depth and to save on heavy calls made on a per-item basis. Where real performance problem arise, however, is when these loops are bound to a collection that evolves asynchronously. Indeed, Angular, and all frameworks allowing these kinds of bindings for that matter, repaint the collection every time it changes. Indeed, it can now show which items inside the collection have been modified and how to select them within the DOM. Consequently, if you have 1,000 elements in a collection, if one of the elements is modified, then the whole collection has to be repainted. In practice, this is quite transparent to both the user and the developer. Nevertheless, selecting and updating 1,000 DOM elements regarding the value of the JavaScript collection is computationally expansive.

Let's simulate a collection of books:

```
export class Book {
   public constructor(public id:number, public title:string){

     this.id = id;
     this.title = title;
   }
}
```

The `Book` class is straightforward. It only contains two properties: `id` and `title`. In the default app component, we add a list of books and a few methods. In the constructor, we populate the books. We also have a refresh method that will randomly select a book and update its title. Finally, the `makeid` method generates a random string ID that we can use to populate the book title:

```
import { Component } from '@angular/core';
import { Book } from './books'
```

```
@Component({
  selector: 'app-root',
  templateUrl: './app.component.html',
  styleUrls: ['./app.component.css']
})
export class AppComponent {
  title = 'app';
  books: Book[] = [];
  constructor(){
    for (let i = 0; i < 10; i++) {
      this.books.push(new Book(i, this.makeid()))
    }
  }
  refresh(){
    let id =Math.floor(Math.random() * this.books.length)
    this.books[id].title = this.makeid();
    console.log(id, "refreshed")
  }
  private makeid(): string {
    var text = "";
    var possible =
"ABCDEFGHIJKLMNOPQRSTUVWXYZabcdefghijklmnopqrstuvwxyz0123456789";
    for (var i = 0; i < 15; i++)
      text += possible.charAt(Math.floor(Math.random() * possible.length));
    return text;
  }
}
```

The last piece of our experiment is the HTML template below:

```
<ul>
  <li *ngFor="let book of books; let i = index">{{book.id}} -
{{book.title}}</li>
</ul>
<button (click)="refresh()">Refresh</button>
```

Our book class, the app component, and the `html` template, when put together, create the following page:

We have our 10 books and our **Refresh** button, which is linked to the `refresh` function. When pressed, one book will be randomly selected and updated. Now, by default, the entire list would have to be recomputed. Of course, the *refresh* mechanism is manual here but, in a more realistic scenario, the refresh will be asynchronous from a remote API update, for example. To help Angular figure out which element has been changed and needs to be refreshed, we can use the `trackBy` option of `ngFor` like so:

```
<ul>
  <li *ngFor="let book of books; trackBy: trackByFn; let i =
index">{{book.id}} - {{book.title}}</li>
</ul>
<button (click)="refresh()">Refresh</button>
The trackBy: trackByFn;we added references a function of our component
named trackByFn
  trackByFn(index, item) {
    return index; // or item.id
  }
```

This function helps Angular know how to track our elements in the book collection. Now, when the **Refresh button** is pressed, only the modified element will be recomputed and repainted. In other words, only one DOM element will be manipulated. Once again, for 10 elements, the difference will not be noticeable. For a few dozen, however, one may start to feel the page become a bit sluggish, depending on one's hardware. We can assert that the trackByFn function operates as intend by using the Chrome development tools. While inspecting the DOM, if you click the **Refresh** button, then only one of the `<li>` markups should light up. DOM elements are lighting up when modified. In the following screenshot, you can see that only the element at index **6** is being recomputed rather than all the elements of the list:

```
<!DOCTYPE html>
<html lang="en" class="gr__localhost">
▶ #shadow-root (open)
▶ <head>…</head>
▼ <body data-gr-c-s-loaded="true">
  ▼ <app-root _nghost-c0 ng-version="5.2.10">
    ▼ <ul _ngcontent-c0>
        <!--bindings={
        "ng-reflect-ng-for-of": "[object Object],[object Object",
        "ng-reflect-ng-for-track-by": "function (index, item) {\r\n      "
        }-->
        <li _ngcontent-c0>0 - PvJtTzYjz0rtzXu</li>
        <li _ngcontent-c0>1 - qb6WbQyiHt1MxB4</li>
        <li _ngcontent-c0>2 - eYRuokSUqVFECET</li>
        <li _ngcontent-c0>3 - ath5Qerx5xlltjb</li>
        <li _ngcontent-c0>4 - c9Aktu3AcUGVIrG</li>
        <li _ngcontent-c0>5 - aQ1LNT0BgvLICY1</li>
        <li _ngcontent-c0>                    </li>
        <li _ngcontent-c0>7 - uGQcTHS5vPERuFu</li> == $0
        <li _ngcontent-c0>8 - ple5EaP7mDCY73W</li>
        <li _ngcontent-c0>9 - bCUAvRgWIDtHCJW</li>
      </ul>
      <button _ngcontent-c0>Refresh</button>
    </app-root>
    <script type="text/javascript" src="inline.bundle.js"></script>
    <script type="text/javascript" src="polyfills.bundle.js"></script>
    <script type="text/javascript" src="styles.bundle.js"></script>
    <script type="text/javascript" src="vendor.bundle.js"></script>
```

Change detection and immutable states

The problem we ealluded to in our previous recipe is inherent to any framework that maps some sort of view and model. It isn't an Angular particularity. That being said, this problem, while exacerbated within loops, also exists in other places. To be precise, it exists everywhere we bind everything between our models and out the view. In other words, every time we have `{{ myValue }}` somewhere in our HTML model, it is a performance hit for our application.

So, what is the solution? Stop using binding altogether? Well, that would not be very practical, as we would give up on what makes JavaScript attractive in the first place. No, the real solution is to make our objects immutable. However, to understand why, we need to take a look at how change detection is achieved in Angular. Change detection is, as its name suggests, the process that Angular performs to detect if anything has changed. If so, the objects are reprocessed and repainted to the DOM. The way Angular does this by default is by attaching a *watcher* to our models. Watchers watch the model and, for each value bound to the view, keeps a few things. It keeps the reference of the bound object, the old value of each property of the object, and the new value of each property of the object. The old and new values are used when the object is changing state. In the book example from the previous section, the watcher for our model would have, for each book, its reference, old and new ID, and old and new title. At each detection cycle, Angular will check if the old and new properties of the object match, as follows:

```
book == book ? No; repaintBook.title == Book.title? No; repaintBook.id ==
Book.it ? No; repaint
```

As usual, taken individually, these actions do not weigh much. However, when having hundreds of objects with dozens of mapped properties within your page, well, you will feel the performance hit. As I said before, the answer to this is immutability. Immutability of objects means that our objects cannot change their properties. If we want to change the values displayed in our view, then we must change the object altogether. If you follow the principle of immutability, then the control flow from before would look like this:

```
book == book ? No; repaint
```

This saves us a lot of ifs and buts everywhere in our application, but it also means that the modification to bound variables in our models such as book.title = "qwerty" will not be reflected in the view. What we will have to do to make this modification visible is feed the view with a new book object. Let's experiment a bit with this new concept. Here's our HTML template:

```
{{ book.id }} - {{ book.title }}<br/><button
(click)="changeMe()">CHANGE</button>
```

And here's our component:

```
import { Component } from '@angular/core';
import { Book } from './book'
@Component({
  selector: 'app-root',
  templateUrl: './app.component.html',
  styleUrls: ['./app.component.css']
})
export class AppComponent {
```

```
  title = 'app';
  book: Book;
  constructor(){
    this.book = new Book(1, "Some Title");
  }
  changeMe(){
    this.book.title = "Some Other Title";
  }
}
```

The book class stays as presented in the previous section. Now, on serving this application, you'll be greeted with the following:

And pressing the **CHANGE** button will change the displayed title, as follows:

If we tell Angular that we would prefer to only check if the references have changed rather than checking for the values of every property by using the ChangeDetection.OnPush method, then the button will not have any effect on the view anymore. Indeed, the value of the model will have been changed, but the change will not have been caught by the change detection algorithm as the reference of the book is still the same, as we explained earlier. Consequently, if you do want to propagate your changes to the view, you have to change the reference. Here's what our component looks like with all this in mind:

```
import { Component, Input } from '@angular/core';
import { Book } from './book'
import { ChangeDetectionStrategy } from '@angular/core';
@Component({
  selector: 'app-root',
  templateUrl: './app.component.html',
  styleUrls: ['./app.component.css'],
  changeDetection: ChangeDetectionStrategy.OnPush
})
export class AppComponent {
  title = 'app';
  @Input() book: Book;
  constructor(){
```

```
      this.book = new Book(1, "Some Title");
    }
    changeMe(){
      this.book = new Book(this.book.id, "Some Other Title");
    }
  }
```

We added `changeDetection: ChangeDetectionStrategy.OnPush` to our component and changed the `changeMe` method so that it creates a new book rather than updating the old one. Of course, creating a new object is more expensive than updating an existing object. However, this technique brings better performance to Angular applications because there are infinitely more cycles where nothing changes, but the properties of each object are still compared to their old values, than cycles where something is actually changed.

With this technique, we significantly improve the performance of our applications to the cost of having to think when we want an update to an object to be propagated to the view. Note that this also applies to filter and pipe. If your application only has a bound value from the model to the view, you might think that it does not matter and you could go mutable all the way. You would be right if your application indeed only had one bonded value, and this value was never piped or filtered using the `{{ myValue | myPipe }}` notation.

Indeed, each pipe is treated asynchronously by our application. In fact, if you have 100 calls to `myPipe`, you are effectively creating the equivalent of 100 watchers that watch the value of `myValue` and will apply your pipe to it. It makes sense because your pipe cannot know what's coming its way and cannot anticipate that the results of its computation will be identical for the 100 calls. Consequently, it watches and executes as many times as needed. If you find yourself with a template filled with a pipe invocation that returns all the same values, you are better off creating a dummy component with that value as input or storing the transformed value in your model altogether.

Prototype and the reusable pool

Object-oriented developers look at ways to reduce the cost of creating objects – especially when those objects are expensive to create because they require, for example, a database pull or complex mathematical operations. Another reason to invest in reducing the creation cost of a particular object is when you create a lot of them. Nowadays, backend developers tend to disregard this aspect of optimization as on-demand CPU/memory have become cheap and easy to adjust. It'll literally cost you a few bucks more a month to have an additional core or 256 MB of RAM on your backend.

This used to be a big deal for desktop application developers too. On a client desktop, there is no way to add CPU/RAM on demand, but fairly cadenced quad cores and a ridiculous amount of RAM for a consumer PC made the issue less problematic. Nowadays, only games and intensive analytics solutions developers seem to care. So, why should you care about the creation time of your object after all? Well, you are building something that is likely to be accessed from old devices (I still use an iPad 1 for casual browsing in the kitchen or on the couch). While desktop application developers can publish minimum and recommended configurations – and enforce them by refusing to install them themselves – we, as web developers, don't have this luxury. Now, if your website doesn't behave properly, users won't question their machines, but your skills... Ultimately, they won't use your products, even when on a capable machine. Let's see how to use the Prototype design pattern. First, we'll need a Prototype interface like so:

```
export interface Prototype{
    clone():Prototype;
}
```

The Prototype interface only defines the clone method that returns a Prototype-compliant object. You've guessed it, the optimized way of creating objects is to clone them when needed! So, let's say you have an object called Movie that, for some reasons, takes time to build:

```
export class Movie implements Prototype {

    private title:string;
    private year:number;
    //...


    public constructor()
    public constructor(title:string = undefined, year:number = undefined)
    {
        if(title == undefined || year == undefined){
            //do the expensive creation
        }else{
            this.title = title;
            this.year = year;
        }
    }

    clone() : Movie {
```

```
            return new Movie(this.title, this.year);
        }
    }

    expansiveMovie:Movie = new Movie();
    cheapMovie = expansiveMovie.clone();
```

As you can see, the way we override functions in TypeScript is different from most languages. Here, the two signatures of the constructor are on top of each other and share the same implementation. And that's it for the `Prototype` pattern. One another pattern that often goes with the `Prototype` pattern is the object pool pattern. While working with expensive-to-create objects, cloning them sure makes a difference. A bigger difference would be to not do anything at all: no creation, no cloning. To achieve this, we can use the pool pattern. In this pattern, we have a pool of objects ready to be shared by any clients or components in the case of an Angular 2 application. The pool implementation is simple:

```
export class MoviePool{
    private static movies:[{movie:Movie, used:boolean}] = [];
    private static nbMaxMovie = 10;
    private static instance:MoviePool;

    private static constructor(){}

    public static getMovie(){

        //first hard create
        if(MoviePool.movies.length == 0){

            MoviePool.movies.push({movie:new User(), used:true});
            return MoviePool.movies[0].movie;

        }else{

            for(var reusableMovie:{movie:Movie, used:boolean} of
MoviePool.movies){
                if(!reusableMovie.used){
                    reusableMovie.used = true;
                    return reusableMovie.movie;
                }
            }
        }

        //subsequent clone create
        if(MoviePool.movie.length < MoviePool.nbMaxMovie){

MoviePool.movies.push({movie:MoviePool.movies[MoviePool.movies.length -
1].clone(), used:true});
```

```
                return MoviePool.movies[MoviePool.movies.length - 1].movie;
        }
        throw new Error('Out of movies');
    }

    public static releaseMovie(movie:Movie){
        for(var reusableMovie:{movie:Movie, used:boolean} of
MoviePool.movies){
            if(reusableMovie.movie === movie){
                reusableMovie.used = false;
            }
            return;
        }
    }
}
```

First and foremost, the pool is also a singleton. Indeed, it wouldn't make much sense to have this costly object reusable design if anyone can create pools at will. Consequently, we have the static `instance:MoviePool` and the private constructor to ensure that only one pool can be created. Then, we have the following attribute: `private static movies:[{movie:Movie, used:boolean}] = [];`.

The `movies` attribute stores a collection of movies and a boolean that determines if anyone is currently using any given movie. As the movie objects are hypothetically taxing to create or maintain in memory, it makes sense to have a hard limit on how many such objects we can have in our pool. This limit is managed by the private static `nbMaxMovie = 10;` attribute. To obtain movies, components would have to call the `getMovie():Movie` method. This method does a hard create on the first movie and then leverages the `Prototype` pattern to create any subsequent movie. Every time a movie is checked out of the pool, the `getMovie` method changes the `used` boolean to true. Note that, in the case where the pool is full and we don't have any free movies to give away, an error is thrown.

Finally, components need a way to check their movies back to the pool so that others can use them. This is achieved by the `releaseMovie` method. This method receives a hypothetically checked-out movie, and iterates over the movies of the pool to set them, according to the boolean, to false. Hence, the movie becomes usable for other components.

Summary

In this chapter, we learned how to avoid major performance pitfalls in our *Angular* application by limiting our AJAX call, and with the proxy design pattern. We also learned how to control the undesirable effects of our loops performance-wise. We then took a dive into the change detection process of Angular to make it work nicely with immutable objects for the times where our object count gets too high. Finally, we also learned about the prototype and reusable pool pattern, which can help in reducing the footprint of our application regarding required resources.

In the next chapter, we will learn about operations patterns for our Angular application. Operations patterns are patterns that help in monitoring and diagnosing live applications.

7
Operation Patterns

In this final chapter, we will focus on patterns to improve the operation of enterprise-scale Angular applications. While the previous chapters focused on stability, performance, and navigation, it might all fall apart if we cannot operate our apps smoothly. While operating your apps, there are several desirable things to consider, such as:

- Transparency
- Logging
- Diagnostics

Now, operations strategies and patterns for backend applications can be easier to implement. While backend applications can run in different flavors of containers, virtual machines, or even barebones, it is easier to operate them compared to frontend applications. Indeed, you can register ongoing procedures, CPU usage, Ram usage, disk usage, and so on, and you can do this because, directly or indirectly (via your service provider), you have access to these servers. For frontend applications, these statistics are still desirable. Let's imagine that we have a frontend application written in Angular that performs well in all regards during our testing, but fails while live. Why would this happen? Well, for example, if you develop Angular applications that are consuming locally deployed APIs, you will have to take into consideration that your users suffer network latencies. These latencies could make your application misbehave.

General health metrics

The first action we can take towards the observability of our Angular application is to monitor some general health metrics. General health metrics that we will be working with are divided into a few categories. First, we have two metrics coming from the Angular profiler:

- `msPerTick`: The average `ms` it took per tick. A tick can be considered a refresh operation or repaint. In other words, the number of milliseconds it takes to repaint all your variables.
- `numTicks`: The number of elapsed ticks.

Other kinds of metrics we collect are related to the client workstation:

- `core`: The number of logical cores
- `appVersion`: The browser used

We can also extract information about the connection:

- `cnxDownlink`: Downlink connection speed
- `cnxEffectiveType`: The connection type

Finally, the last set of metrics deals with the heap size of JavaScript itself:

- `jsHeapSizeLimit`: The max size of the heap.
- `totalJSHeapSize`: This is the current size of the JavaScript heap, including free space not occupied by any JavaScript objects. This means that `usedJsHeapSize` cannot be greater than `totalJsHeapSize`.
- `usedJSHeapSize`: Total amount of memory being used by JavaScript objects including V8 internal objects.

In order to collect these metrics, we will create a dedicated Angular service. This service will be in charge of accessing the right variables, assembling them into a perfect object, and sending them back to our infrastructure with an API post.

The first set of metrics is accessible via the Angular profiler. The profiler is injecting a variable named `ng` that is accessible via your browser command line. Most tools that can be used to monitor Angular application performances are used while developing them. In order to access this, we can use the `window` variable and grab it like so:

```
window["ng"].profiler
```

Then, we have access to the `timeChangeDetection` method, which provides us with the `msPerTick` and `numTicks` metrics.

Within a method, this translates to the following:

```
var timeChangeDetection = window["ng"].profiler.timeChangeDetection()
```

Another useful variable that can be found in any JavaScript application is the navigator. The navigator variable, as its name suggests, exposes information about the browser used by our users. `window.navigator.hardwareConcurrency` and `window.navigator.appVersion` give us the number of logical cores and the app version, respectively.

While the previously mentioned variables are accessible on any browser capable of running an *Angular* app, the rest of the metrics are, at the time of writing, only available on Chrome. If our users use something other than Chrome, then we will not have access to these metrics. Chrome, however, is still the most used browser, and there is no sign that this will change anytime soon. Consequently, for a large portion of our user base, we will be able to retrieve them.

The next batch of metrics are the ones related to the memory performances of our applications: `jsHeapSizeLimit`, `totalJSHeapSize`, and `usedJSHeapSize`. On Chrome, they are properties of the `window.performance["memory"]` object. For other browsers, however, we need to provide a polyfill:

```
var memory:any = window.performance["memory"] ?
window.performance["memory"] : {
"jsHeapSizeLimit":0,
"totalJSHeapSize":0,
"usedJSHeapSize":0,
}
```

In the preceding code, we check for the existence of the `memory` object. If the object exists, we assign it to the local `memory` variable. If the object does not exist, we provide a trivial polyfill that has 0-valued metrics.

The last set of metrics are the ones related to the connection of our user. Like the memory object, it is only accessible on Chrome. We will use the same technique as before:

```
var connection:any = window.navigator["connection"] ?
window.navigator["connection"] : {
"effectiveType": "n/a",
"cnxDownlink": 0,
}
```

Here is the implementation of the `Monitor` service with the gathering of the metrics inside the `metric` method. At the end of the method, we send the metrics to an API endpoint:

```
import { Injectable } from '@angular/core';
import { HttpClient } from '@angular/common/http';
@Injectable()
export class MonitorService {
constructor(private http:HttpClient) { }
public metrics(){
var timeChangeDetection = window["ng"].profiler.timeChangeDetection()
var memory:any = window.performance["memory"] ?
window.performance["memory"] : {
"jsHeapSizeLimit":0,
"totalJSHeapSize":0,
"usedJSHeapSize":0,
}
var connection:any = window.navigator["connection"] ?
window.navigator["connection"] : {
"effectiveType": "n/a",
"cnxDownlink": 0,
}
var perf = {
"msPerTick": timeChangeDetection.msPerTick,
"numTicks": timeChangeDetection.numTicks,
"core": window.navigator.hardwareConcurrency,
"appVersion": window.navigator.appVersion,
"jsHeapSizeLimit": memory.jsHeapSizeLimit,
"totalJSHeapSize": memory.totalJSHeapSize,
"usedJSHeapSize": memory.usedJSHeapSize,
"cnxEffectiveType": connection.effectiveType,
"cnxDownlink": connection.downlink,
}
this.http.post("https://api.yourwebsite/metrics/", perf)
return perf;
}
}
```

Here is an example of the variables within the `perf` object:

- `msPerTick`: 0.0022148688576149405
- `numTicks`: 225747
- `core`: 12

- appVersion: 5.0 (Windows NT 10.0; Win64; x64) AppleWebKit/537....L, like Gecko) Chrome/66.0.3359.139 Safari/537.36" jsHeapSizeLimit: 2190000000, ...}appVersion: "5.0 (Windows NT 10.0; Win64; x64) AppleWebKit/537.36 (KHTML, like Gecko) Chrome/66.0.3359.139 Safari/537.36
- cnxDownlink: 10
- cnxEffectiveType: 4g
- core: 12
- jsHeapSizeLimit: 2190000000
- msPerTick: 0.0022148688576149405
- numTicks: 225747
- totalJSHeapSize: 64000000
- usedJSHeapSize: 56800000

On the server side, these metrics can be fed into an ELK stack or something similar of your choosing and enhance the observability of your application.

Specific metrics

In addition to the metric we looked at earlier, we can add a method in our service so that we are able to send specific metrics, like so:

```
public metric(label:string, value:any){
this.http.post("https://api.yourwebsite/metric/", {
label:label,
value:value,
})
}
```

Error reporting

Another way to enhance the transparency and observability of your application is to report each and every JavaScript error that occurs on the client side. Doing so is relatively simple in JavaScript; you simply need to attach a callback function to the `window.onerror` event, as follows:

```
window.onerror = function myErrorHandler(errorMsg, url, lineNumber) {
alert("Error occured: " + errorMsg);
}
```

This will simply create an alert each time an error occurs. With Angular, however, you cannot use the same simple technique—not because it is complicated, but because it requires the creation of the ne class. This new class will implement the Angular error handler interface like so:

```
class MyErrorHandler implements ErrorHandler {
handleError(error) {
// do something with the exception
}
}
```

We will continue to improve upon the `monitor` service so that it can also be our `ErrorHandler`:

```
import { Injectable, ErrorHandler } from '@angular/core';
import { HttpClient } from '@angular/common/http';
@Injectable()
export class MonitorService implements ErrorHandler{
constructor(private http:HttpClient) { }
handleError(error) {
this.http.post("https://api.yourwebsite/errors/", error)
}
...
}
```

Then, these errors can be fed to your ELK stack or even plugged in directly to your Slack channel, as we do at `Toolwatch.io`:

For this error handler to be used in place of Angular's default one, you need to provide it when declaring your modules:

```
providers : [{ provide : ErrorHandler, useClass : MonitorService }]
```

Method metrics with AOP

As of now, we only managed to monitor our system with specific moments: calls to metrics, metrics, and errors occurring. A sure way to monitor everything in our application is to use **AOP (Aspect-oriented programming)** within our *Angular* apps. AOP is not a new technique, but it isn't widely used in the JavaScript ecosystem. AOP consists of defining aspects. Aspects are subprograms that are associated with specified pieces of our application. Aspects are woven into methods at compilation time and are executed before and/or after the method they are woven into. In the case of Angular-based applications, the method will be woven at transpilation from TypeScript to JavaScript. Weaving an aspect to a method in vanilla JavaScript is simple. Consider the following example:

```
function myFunc(){
Console.log("hello");
}
function myBeforeAspect(){
Console.log("before...")
}
function myAfterAspect(){
Console.log("after");
}
var oldFunc = myFunc;
myFunc = function(){
myBeforeAspect();
oldFunc();
myAfterAspect();
}
```

In this snippet, we declare three functions: `myBeforeAspect`, `myFunc`, and `myAfterAspect`. After their respective declarations, we create the `oldFunc` variable and assign it to `myFunc`. Then, we replace the implementation of `myFunc` with a new implementation. In this new implementation, we call `myBeforeAspect` and `myAfterAspect` in addition to `oldFunc`. This is a simple way of doing aspects in JavaScript. We have behaviors that have been added to the call of `myFunc` without breaking our internal API. Indeed, if in another part of the program we called the `myFunc` function, then our program would still be valid and would execute as if nothing had changed. In addition, we can continue to add other aspects to the augmented function.

This is also achievable in Angular-flavored TypeScript:

```
constructor(){
this.click = function(){
this.before();
this.click();
this.after();
```

```
}
}
after(){
console.log("after")
}
before(){
console.log("before");
}
click(){
console.log("hello")
}
```

Here, our constructor wove two aspects into the click method. The click method will execute its behavior in addition to that of the aspect. In the HTML, nothing about the AOP transpires:

```
<button (click)="click()">click</button>
```

Now, we could apply this technique manually to all our methods, and call the metric method of our monitoring service. Fortunately, various libraries exist that can handle this for us. The best one to date is called aspect.js (https://github.com/mgechev/aspect.js).

aspect.js leverages the decorator pattern of ECMAScript 2016.

We can install it using npm install aspect.js –save, and then we can define an aspect like so:

```
class LoggerAspect {
@afterMethod({
classNamePattern: /^someClass/,
methodNamePattern: /^(some|other)/
})
invokeAfterMethod(meta: Metadata) {
console.log(`Inside of the logger. Called
${meta.className}.${meta.method.name} with args: ${meta.method.args.join(',
')}.`);
@beforeMethod({
classNamePattern: /^someClass/,
methodNamePattern: /^(get|set)/
})
invokeBeforeMethod(meta: Metadata) {
console.log(`Inside of the logger. Called
${meta.className}.${meta.method.name} with args: ${meta.method.args.join(',
')}.`);
}
}
```

In this aspect, we have several parts. First, we have the `@afterMethod` method which takes a `classNamePattern` and a `methodNamePattern`. These patterns are regular expressions and are used to define which classes and methods are woven into that particular aspect. Then, in `invokeAfterMethod`, we define the behavior we want to apply. In this method, we simply log the method that was called and the argument values with which said method was invoked.

We repeat this operation with `@beforeMethod`.

If we were to keep things like this, the log would be printed out on the client side. If we want to get hold of these logs, we will have to modify our `Monitor` service once again.

We will add a static method called `log` and a static `HTTP` client. These are static because we will likely weave components that do not receive an injection of the `Monitor` service. This way, all services, with or without injection, will be able to send their logs:

```
static httpStatic:HttpClient
constructor(private http:HttpClient) {
MonitorService.httpStatic = http;
}
static sendLog(log:string){
MonitorService.httpStatic.post("https://api.yourwebsite/logs/", log)
}
```

In the constructor of the `Monitor` service, we populate the static client. This will be done as soon as our applications boot up and the services are singleton. Consequently, we do this only once.

Here is the complete implementation of the `Monitor` service:

```
import { Injectable, ErrorHandler } from '@angular/core';
import { HttpClient } from '@angular/common/http';
@Injectable()
export class MonitorService implements ErrorHandler{
static httpStatic:HttpClient
constructor(private http:HttpClient) {
MonitorService.httpStatic = http;
}
public static log(log:string){
MonitorService.httpStatic.post("https://api.yourwebsite/logs/", log)
}
handleError(error) {
this.http.post("https://api.yourwebsite/metrics/", error)
}
public metric(label:string, value:any){
this.http.post("https://api.yourwebsite/metric/", {
```

```
label:label,
value:value,
})
}
public metrics(){
var timeChangeDetection = window["ng"].profiler.timeChangeDetection()
var memory:any = window.performance["memory"] ?
window.performance["memory"] : {
"jsHeapSizeLimit":0,
"totalJSHeapSize":0,
"usedJSHeapSize":0,
}
var connection:any = window.navigator["connection"] ?
window.navigator["connection"] : {
"effectiveType": "n/a",
"cnxDownlink": 0,
}
this.metric("msPerTick", timeChangeDetection.msPerTick);
this.metric("numTicks", timeChangeDetection.numTicks);
this.metric("core", window.navigator.hardwareConcurrency);
this.metric("appVersion", window.navigator.appVersion);
this.metric("jsHeapSizeLimit", memory.jsHeapSizeLimit);
this.metric("totalJSHeapSize", memory.totalJSHeapSize);
this.metric("usedJSHeapSize", memory.usedJSHeapSize);
this.metric("cnxEffectiveType", connection.effectiveType);
this.metric("cnxDownlink", connection.downlink);
}
}
```

The aspect can be modified to call the new static method:

```
class LoggerAspect {
@afterMethod({
classNamePattern: /^SomeClass/,
methodNamePattern: /^(some|other)/
})
invokeBeforeMethod(meta: Metadata) {
MonitorService.log(`Called ${meta.className}.${meta.method.name} with args:
${meta.method.args.join(', ')}.`);
}
@beforeMethod({
classNamePattern: /^SomeClass/,
methodNamePattern: /^(get|set)/
})
invokeBeforeMethod(meta: Metadata) {
MonitorService.log(`Inside of the logger. Called
${meta.className}.${meta.method.name} with args: ${meta.method.args.join(',
')}.`);
```

```
}
}
```

In addition to `className`, `methodName`, and `args`, we can populate the meta variable of each component with the `@Wove` syntax, as shown in the following code:

```
@Wove({ bar: 42, foo : "bar" })
class SomeClass { }
```

An interesting use case of the custom meta variables is to use them to store the execution time of each method, as the meta variable value is carried from the before to the after method.

Consequently, we could have a variable called `startTime` in our `@Wove` annotation and use it like this:

```
@Wove({ startTime: 0 })
class SomeClass { }
class ExecutionTimeAspect {
@afterMethod({
classNamePattern: /^SomeClass/,
methodNamePattern: /^(some|other)/
})
invokeBeforeMethod(meta: Metadata) {
meta.startTime = Date.now();
}
@beforeMethod({
classNamePattern: /^SomeClass/,
methodNamePattern: /^(get|set)/
})
invokeBeforeMethod(meta: Metadata) {
MonitorService.metric(`${meta.className}.${meta.method.name`,
Date.now() - meta.startTime;
}
}
```

Now, we have another aspect that will be woven into our class, which will measure its execution time and report it with the `metric` method of `MonitorService`.

Summary

Operating Angular applications can be complex, because it is relatively hard to observe our applications when they are running. While observing backend applications is straightforward, because we have access to the running environment, the techniques we are used to cannot be applied directly. In this chapter, we saw how to have an Angular application monitor itself by using collection performance metrics, custom metrics, and logs, and applied all of this automatically by using aspect-oriented programming.

While the techniques exposed in this chapter can provide 100% observability of your applications, they have also some drawbacks. Indeed, if your applications are popular, you will be overcharging your backend infrastructure not only to serve your pages and answer your API calls, but to accepts logs and metrics. Another drawback is that ill-intentioned people could feed you bad metrics via your APIs and provide you with a biased picture of what is currently happening within your live applications.

These drawbacks can be addressed by only monitoring a subset of your clients. For example, you could activate logging and tracing for only 5% of your clients based on a randomly generated number. In addition, you could verify the authenticity of the users that want to send you metrics by providing CSRF tokens for each request.

Other Books You May Enjoy

If you enjoyed this book, you may be interested in these other books by Packt:

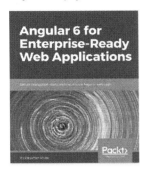

Angular 6 for Enterprise-Ready Web Applications
Doguhan Uluca

ISBN: 978-1-78646-290-9

- Create full-stack web applications using Angular and RESTful APIs
- Master Angular fundamentals, RxJS, CLI tools, unit testing, GitHub, and Docker
- Design and architect responsive, secure and scalable apps to deploy on AWS
- Adopt a minimalist, value-first approach to delivering your app with Kanban
- Get introduced to automated testing with continuous integration on CircleCI
- Optimize Nginx and Node.js web servers with load testing tools

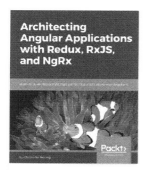

Architecting Angular Applications with Redux, RxJS, and NgRx
Christoffer Noring

ISBN: 978-1-78712-240-6

- Understand the one-way data flow and Flux pattern
- Work with functional programming and asynchronous data streams
- Figure out how RxJS can help us address the flaws in promises
- Set up different versions of cascading calls
- Explore advanced operators
- Get familiar with the Redux pattern and its principles
- Test and debug different features of your application
- Build your own lightweight app using Flux, Redux, and NgRx

Leave a review - let other readers know what you think

Please share your thoughts on this book with others by leaving a review on the site that you bought it from. If you purchased the book from Amazon, please leave us an honest review on this book's Amazon page. This is vital so that other potential readers can see and use your unbiased opinion to make purchasing decisions, we can understand what our customers think about our products, and our authors can see your feedback on the title that they have worked with Packt to create. It will only take a few minutes of your time, but is valuable to other potential customers, our authors, and Packt. Thank you!

Index

Printed in Great Britain
by Amazon